Revising
Prose

FIFTH EDITION

Richard A. Lanham
University of California, Los Angeles

PEARSON
Longman

New York   Boston   San Francisco
London   Toronto   Sydney   Tokyo   Singapore   Madrid
Mexico City   Munich   Paris   Cape Town   Hong Kong   Montreal

Senior Sponsoring Editor: Virginia L. Blanford
Senior Marketing Manager: Sandra McGuire
Production Manager: Donna DeBenedictis
Project Coordination, Text Design, and Electronic Page Makeup:
  GGS Book Services
Senior Cover Designer/Manager: Nancy Danahy
Senior Manufacturing Buyer: Dennis J. Para

Library of Congress Cataloging-in-Publication Data

Lanham, Richard A.
    Revising prose / Richard A. Lanham. — 5th ed.
        p. cm.
    Includes index.
    ISBN 0-321-44169-9
        1. English language—Rhetoric. 2. English language—Style. 3. Editing.
    I. Title.

PE1421.L297 2006
808'.042—dc22

                                                          2006043294

Please visit us at www.ablongman.com

ISBN 0-321-44169-9

CONTENTS

PREFACE

Revising Prose differs from other writing texts. Let me emphasize these differences up front.

1. About *revising*. True to its title, it is about *revising*; it does not deal with original composition. People often argue that writing cannot be taught, and if they mean that inspiration cannot be commanded nor laziness banished, then of course they are right. But stylistic analysis—revision—is something else, a method, not a mystical rite. How we compose—pray for the muse, marshal our thoughts, find willpower to glue backside to chair—may be idiosyncratic, but revision belongs to the public domain. Anyone can learn it. But the learning requires some guidance, and this guidance *Revising Prose* provides. It does not tell the whole story but it does tell you how to begin.

In colleges and universities, revising is more common nowadays than it was when this book first appeared in 1979. Computers have made it easier to do. Still, except in composition classes, instructors seldom require it or help students revise on their own. Nothing would improve student writing—or student thinking—more than steady, detailed revision. In the workplace to which school leads, revision usually poses more problems than original composition. At work the "student's dilemma," what to write about, hardly exists. The facts are there, the needs press hard, the arguments lie ready to hand, the deadline impends. The first draft assembles itself from the external pressures. You bat it out on a crowded plane flying home from a meeting. Or start with the draft a colleague has batted out. Then the sweat really begins: *revision*, commonly done in group settings. For much organizational writing, collective revision up through a hierarchy determines the final text. "All writing is rewriting," goes the cliché. OK. Here's the book for it. It offers a collective writing philosophy that a group can easily and quickly learn to share.

2. Translates the "Official Style" into English. A specific analytical and social premise informs *Revising Prose*: Much bad writing today comes not from the conventional sources of verbal dereliction—sloth, ignorance, or native absence of mind—but from stylistic imitation. It is learned, an act of stylistic piety which imitates a single style, the bureaucratic style I call the Official Style. This bureaucratic style dominates written discourse in our time, and beginning or harried or fearful writers adopt it as a protective coloration. So common a writing pattern deserves a separate focus, a book of its own. *Revising Prose* is about revising the Official Style into plain English.

I once thought that the Official Style might be going out of style. Not so. It moves from strength to strength. It started as the language of bureaucratic officials, and reaches back as far as bureaucracy does, which is as far back as the human record goes. Writing itself may have been invented to keep bureaucratic accounts. The language of the law took on an Official Style coloration as soon as law became a profession. A variation of the Official Style has now suffused business writing and talk and—with special zest—the academic conversation. As the world has become bureaucratized, so has its language.

This colonization has not gone unnoticed or unprotested, both in print and on the Internet. Even the government, the *fons et origo*, the fountain and source, of the Official Style, has chimed in. The Securities and Exchange Commission has started requiring that initial public offerings in new companies be written in a plain style. In 1998, President Clinton issued an executive order instructing federal agencies to communicate in writing that is "clearer and easier to understand." Maybe this miracle will come to pass, but don't expect every "personal flotational device" to turn back into a "lifejacket" overnight. If you are a bureaucrat who wants to take the executive order to heart, though, *Revising Prose* is just the book for you.

3. Rule-based and self-teaching. *Revising Prose* was written as a supplementary text for any course or task that requires writing. The pressures of school or workplace rarely permit time off to take a special writing course. You need something useful right now. Again, a special book for this purpose seems justified. Because it addresses a single discrete style, *Revising Prose* can be *rule-based* to a degree that prose analysis rarely permits. This set of rules—the Paramedic Method (PM)—in turn allows the book to be self-teaching.

4. Useful in all jobs. Because the Official Style now dominates university, workplace, and government alike, *Revising Prose* can work in all these contexts. It addresses the revising self in all of us. That revising self is neither the writing self nor the reading self, but a third one which uneasily combines both. Scholars who study children's language have argued that language-understanding and language-using evolve as separate systems, which only later combine into full language competence. Revising tries to hold these two different powers, two different selves, in mind at once. That's what makes it so hard. In my experience, the land of revision is an egalitarian place where pedagogical authority gives way to common perplexity. Thus *Revising Prose* addresses a general audience. Used as directed, the Paramedic Method works for anyone.

5. Addresses the *electronic* word. If writing on an electronic screen has revolutionized prose composition and prose style, nowhere has the revolution hit harder than in revision. Revision is easier to do on screen than on a page, and *Revising Prose* suggests some ways to have more fun doing it.

6. Saves time and money when used as directed. Bottom line: The Paramedic Method, when used as directed, saves time and money. Lots of it. Word-processing time, fax time, duplicating time, file space (the paperless office of the future remains in the future), reading time, and, above all, thinking time. The lard factor of the Official Style usually runs about 50% and eliminating it generates equivalent savings in all these areas. We live now in an economy where attention is the scarce commodity. The quicker we cut to the chase, the quicker we catch our meaning.

But this book envisions an even more powerful efficiency: stylistic self-consciousness. This verbal self-awareness, however generated, is like riding a bicycle. Once learned, never forgotten; you can ride it wherever you want to go. Stylistic self-consciousness changes how we read and write not only in a single bureaucratic register but across the board. Such a skill has moral implications, implications dealt with in the last chapter, "Why Bother?"

7. Sentence-based. The last point and the most important. _Revising Prose_ focuses on the single sentence. Get the basic architecture of the English sentence straight, and everything else will follow. Transposed up an octave toward generality, this book might have been called _The English Sentence_. We're analyzing in this book the microeconomics of prose. A single sentence constitutes an economy in miniature; our work together will analyze this economy. Such close-focus work is as seldom performed as it is universally needed. We spend so much time worrying about our verbal "P's and Q's" that we ought to spend worrying about sentence economics.

I call my revision procedure the Paramedic Method because it provides emergency therapy, a first-aid kit, a quick, self-teaching method of revision for people who want to translate the Official Style, their own or someone else's, into plain English. But it is only that—a first-aid kit. It's not the art of medicine. As with paramedicine in underdeveloped countries, it does not attempt to teach a full body of knowledge but only to diagnose and cure the epidemic disease. It won't answer, though at the end it addresses, the big question: Having the cure, how do you know when, or if, you should take it? For this you need the full art of prose medicine, a mature and reflective training in verbal self-awareness.

To get the most out of _Revising Prose_, follow the PM. It works only if you _follow_ it rather than _argue_ with it. When it tells you to get rid of the prepositional phrases, get rid of them. Don't go into a "but, well, in this case, given my style, really I need to . . . " bob and weave. You'll never learn anything that way. The PM constitutes the center of this book. Use it. It is printed on a separate page in the front. Copy it and tack it above your desk for easy reference.

8. What's new? *Revising Prose* has been out working in the world for a quarter century now. Readers will want to know what is new in the fifth edition. First and foremost, I've conflated two books, *Revising Prose* and *Revising Business Prose*, into one. I've done this because business prose has become a dialect of the Official Style rather than a separate style. Separate treatment no longer seemed required.

Second, I've reorganized the chapter structure.

Third, I've substantially rewritten much of the text and used many new examples.

Fourth, I've added some parodies of the Official Style here and there to liven things up.

Fifth, I've included some exercises at the end of the book. Most of these are included in the DVD (see below), but a few are new. Try your hand at a couple when you need a break from seeing me revise.

9. The *Revising Prose* DVD. Not long after the first edition of *Revising Prose* was published I wrote a video script to accompany it and UCLA, bless its heart, found the $30,000 to make the video. I narrated it but it did not depict me as a talking head, or leaning on a mantelpiece looking philosophic or—for drama— walking over to a blackboard. Instead, it featured something which until that time had not been used (or, for all I know, even invented): kinetic text, text that moved around on the screen, changed color, beeped with mini-Moog early computer sounds.

This short (28 minutes) video has proved a great success. It is used across America in school and college campuses and in many business and government organizations. In 2004, my friend Michael Cohen and I transferred the video to a DVD, and in two forms: first, the original video running uninterrupted; second, the video divided into ten chapters so that each chapter can be viewed separately. The DVD is available from CustomFlix Online (http://www.customflix.com/206256) for $75. We also put on the DVD the Interactive Exercises formerly available on floppy disks (remember them?) for both *Revising Prose* and *Revising Business Prose*. These include some suggested revisions.

P.S. In case you've forgotten what "active" and "passive," or even "noun" and "verb," mean, I've provided an appendix that defines the grammatical and rhetorical terms used in the text.

R. A. L.

THE PARAMEDIC METHOD

1. Circle the prepositions.

2. Circle the "is" forms.

3. Find the *action*.

4. Put this action in a simple (not compound) active verb.

5. Start fast—no slow windups.

6. Read the passage aloud with emphasis and feeling.

7. Write out each sentence on a blank screen or sheet of paper and mark off its basic rhythmic units with a "/."

8. Mark off sentence length with a "/."

1

Action

Since we all live in a bureaucracy these days, it's not surprising that we end up writing like bureaucrats. Nobody feels comfortable writing simply "Bill loves Marge." The system requires something like "A romantic relationship is ongoing between Bill and Marge." Or "Bill and Marge are currently implementing an interactive romantic relationship." Or still better, "One can easily see that an interactive romantic relationship is currently being fulfilled between Bill and Marge." Ridiculous contrived examples? Here are some real ones.

A businessman denied a loan does not suffer but instead says that "I went through a suffering process." A teacher does not say that "If you use a calculator in class, you will never learn to add and subtract," but instead "The fact is that the use of the calculator in the classroom is negative for the learning process." An undergraduate wants to say that "Every UCLA freshman needs to learn how to cope with crowds," but it comes out as "There can be little doubt that contending with the problem of overpopulation at UCLA is one thing that every freshman needs to learn how to do." A favorite Official Style habit adds "process" or "situation" or "factor" to every phrase. Instead of being invited "to recruit," a corporation is asked "to participate in the recruitment process." Instead of facing "a budget crunch," an administrator faces "a budget crunch situation." "Greed" becomes "the greed factor." Sometimes the inflation is pure air, a "gunfire weapon" for a "gun." A sign outside a courtroom reads not "No guns in court!" but "Firearms may not be brought into this court facility." A university bureaucrat wants to make a generous offer: "To encourage broadband system use, the ACAD will pay all line charges for the next two years." But instead, it comes out as: "In order to stimulate utilization of the broadband system, it is the intention of the ACAD to provide for central funding of all monthly line charges generated by attachment to the system over the period of the next two years." A politician "indicates his reluctance to accept the terms on which the proposal was offered" when he might have said "No." A teacher of business writing tells us not that "People entering business today must learn to speak effectively," but "One of these factors is the seemingly increasing awareness of the idea that to succeed in business, it is imperative that the young person entering a business career possess definite skill in oral communication." A French art historian talking about prehistoric cave wall paintings inflates them into "parietal representations" (Latin *paries* = "wall").

All these people write, and maybe even think, in the Official Style. The Official Style comes in many dialects—government, military, social scientific, lab scientific, MBA flapdoodle—but all exhibit the same basic attributes. They all build on the same imbalance: a dominance of nouns and an atrophy of verbs. They enshrine the triumph, worshipped in every bureaucracy, of stasis over action. Real actions lurk furtively in the sentences I've just quoted—suffer, learn, cope, recruit, pay, speak—but they are swamped by lame "is" verbs, "shun" words (facilitation, intention, utilization), and strings of prepositional phrases.

This basic imbalance between action and inertia is easy to cure, if you want to cure it—and this book's Paramedic Method tells you how to do it. *But when do you want to cure it?* We all sometimes feel, whatever setting we write in, that we will be penalized for writing in plain English. It will sound too flip. Unserious. Even satirical. In my academic dialect, that of literary study, writing plain English nowadays is tantamount to walking down the hall naked as a jay bird. Public places demand protective coloration; sometimes you must write in the Official Style. And when you do, how do you make sure you are writing a good

Official Style—if there is one—rather than a bad one? What can "good" and "bad" mean when applied to prose in this way?

Revising Prose starts out by teaching you how to revise the Official Style. But after you've learned that, we'll reflect on what such revision is likely to do for you, or to you, in the bureaucratic world of the future—and the future is going to get only more bureaucratic, however many efforts we make to simplify it and its official language. You ought then to be able to see what "good" and "bad" mean for prose, and what you are doing when you revise it. And that means you will know how to socialize your revisory talents, how to put them, like your sentences, into action.

PREPOSITIONAL-PHRASE STRINGS

We can begin with three examples of student prose:

> This sentence is in need of an active verb.
>
> Physical satisfaction is the most obvious of the consequences of premarital sex.
>
> In response to the issue of equality for educational and occupational mobility, it is my belief that a system of inequality exists in the school system.

What do they have in common? They have been assembled from strings of prepositional phrases glued together by that all-purpose epoxy "is." In each case the sentence's verbal force has been shunted into a noun, and its verbal force has been diluted into "is," the neutral copulative, the weakest verb in the language. Such sentences project no life, no vigor. They just "are." And the "is" generates those strings of prepositional phrases fore and aft. It's so easy to fix. Look for the real action. Ask yourself, who's kicking who? (Yes, I know, it should be *whom*, but doesn't *whom* sound stilted? In this book, we'll stick with *who*.)

In "This sentence is in need of an active verb," the action obviously lies in "need." And so, "This sentence needs an active verb." The needless prepositional phrase "in need of" simply disappears once we realize who's kicking who. The sentence, animated by a real verb, comes alive, and in six words instead of nine.

Where's the action in "Physical satisfaction is the most obvious of the consequences of premarital sex"? Buried down there in "satisfaction." But just asking the question reveals other problems. Satisfaction isn't a consequence of premarital sex, in the same way that, say, pregnancy can be. And, as generations of both sexes will attest, sex, premarital or otherwise, does not always satisfy. Beyond all this, the contrast between the clinical phrasing of the sentence, with its lifeless "is" verb, and the life-giving power of lust in action makes the sentence seem almost funny. Excavating the action from "satisfaction" yields "Premarital sex satisfies! Obviously!" This gives us a lard factor (LF) of 66% and a comedy factor even higher. (You find the LF by dividing the difference between the number of words in the original and the revision by the number of words in the original. In this case, $12 - 4 = 8$; $8 \div 12 = .66$. Think of a LF of one third to one half as normal, and in your own writing don't stop revising until you've removed it. The comedy factor in prose revision, though often equally great, does not lend itself to numerical calculation.)

But how else do we revise here? "Premarital sex is fun, obviously" may be a little better, but we remain in thrall to "is." And the frequent falsity of the observation stands out yet more. Revision has exposed the empty thinking. The writer makes it even worse by continuing: "Some degree of physical satisfaction is present in almost all coitus." Add it all together and we get something like, "People usually enjoy premarital sex" (LF 79%). Right. At its worst, academic prose makes us laugh by describing ordinary reality in extraordinary language.

Now for the third example.

> In response to the issue of equality for educational and occupational mobility, it is my belief that a system of inequality exists in the school system.

A diagram reveals the problem and points to a lurking action.

In response
to the issue
of equality
for educational and occupational mobility,

it **is** my belief that a system

of inequality exists
in the school system.

A string of prepositional phrases, then a form of the verb "to be" (usually "is"), then more prepositional phrases. But sandwiched in the middle lurks, furtive and afraid, the real *action* of the sentence: "it is my belief that." Change that from the "is" form to the active voice, and we have *an action*. Somebody *believes* something. Everything before and after this action amounts to a single phrase—"gender inequality." So we have this revision.

I believe that gender inequality exists in the schools. (9 words instead of 26; LF 65%)

The drill for this problem stands clear. Circle every form of "to be" (*is, was, will be, seems to be, have been,* etc.) and every prepositional phrase (*of, in, by, through, from,* etc.). Then find out who's kicking who and start rebuilding the sentence with that action. Two prepositional phrases in a row turn on the warning light, three make a problem, and four demand immediate surgery. Look for the real *action* hidden behind the "is" and prepositional phrases. So here:

Original:
The history **of** new regulatory provisions **is** that there **is** generally an immediate resistance **to** them.

What hides behind "is that there is"? *Resistance.* And behind that? *Resist!* Now we need an *actor.* We have to invent one, but clearly "people in general" are acting here. So:

Revision:
People usually resist new regulations.

Five words instead of 16, for a LF of 69%. The two original prepositional phrases have been eliminated. The action—*resist*—stands clear. A little practice in this kind of revision and, instead of writing "There are many ways in which people resist change," you'll write "People resist change in many ways."

The action lies in an even deeper grave of prepositions in this example:

> The project is likely to result in a minor population increase in the city from families relocating to the site from outside the community.

Chart first:

> The project
> **is** likely
> **to** result
> **in** a minor population increase
> **in** the city
> **from** families relocating
> **to** the site
> **from** outside the community.

The classic Official Style formula: an "is," an infinitive "to" phrase, then five prepositional phrases in a row. For once, we have a clear actor—"The project." We'll start there. What is the project *doing?* What verb would express "a minor population increase from outside the city to inside the city"? How about "attract"? What is being "attracted"? Families. It all falls into place.

Revision:
The project will probably attract new families to the city.

Good work: (1) 24 words cut down to 5, for a LF of 58%; (2) five prepositional phrases and one infinitive phrase shrunk to one prepositional phrase; (3) above all, a clearly defined *action*—"attract."

Sometimes authors go to grotesque lengths to hide the action from their readers. Look at an undergraduate disqualifying himself or herself from membership in a creative writing class: "The type of writing that I have an interest in is in the area of creative writing." To get into the class, write instead "I want to study creative writing" (17 words into 6: LF 66%).

Or take this simple example:

Original:
There are several examples of this selection process present in the Listerine ad.

Revision:
The Listerine ad exemplifies this selection process.

Sometimes potential actions are smeared across the whole sentence. Here's a favorite of mine:

Original:
These are disturbed habitats (e.g., roadsides, vacant lots) vegetated by weedy colonizing species which depend on repeated disturbances for their existence.

The Official Style is at its silliest in describing ordinary things like weeds. It just can't stand giving them their plain, ordinary names. A weed has to become "a weedy colonizing species." Now, where's the action? Well, we have a choice:

disturb
vegetate
colonize
depend
disturb [again]
exist

Which offers the central action? None of them. There *isn't any* central action. My guess is that the central, though unexpressed, *action* amounts to this:

Revision:
Weeds *grow* faster in empty spaces.

If I have guessed right, we've reduced 21 words to 6, for a LF of 71%. Not bad for government work. Now another Official Style smear job:

> Perception is the process of extracting information from stimulation emanating from the objects, places, and events in the world around us.

A diagram helps:

> Perception
> **is** the process
> **of** extracting information
> **from** stimulation emanating
> **from** the objects, places, and events
> **in** the world
> **around** us.

Again, look at the possible actions:

> *perceive*
> *process*
> *extract*
> *inform*
> *stimulate*
> *emanate*

Actor is clear, and *action*, too: "Perception extracts information." The rest of the sentence goes into a single prepositional phrase: "from the outside world."

Revision:
Perception extracts information from the outside world.

Profound? No. Clear? Yes. Instead of 21 words, 7, for a LF of 66% exactly. And a five-to-one prepositional-phrase kill ratio.

Sometimes in revision you want so badly to emphasize the central action that you ruthlessly cut away surrounding details.

Next, a sentence from an environmental impact statement:

> Pelicans may also be vulnerable to direct oiling, but the lack of mortality data despite numerous spills in areas frequented by the species suggests that it practices avoidance.

You want to dig out the "avoid" in the Official Style "practices avoidance." And it is clear who is doing the avoiding: the pelicans. So this:

Revision:
Pelicans seem to survive oil spills by avoiding the oil.

Have I left out anything essential in getting from 28 words to 10 (LF 64%)?

Official Style sentences smother action the way foam puts out a fire. Look at these strings from a lawyer, a scientist, and an historian:

> Here **is** an example *of* the use *of* the rule *of* justice *in* argumentation.

> One *of* the most important results *of* the presentation *of* the data **is** the alteration *of* the status *of* the elements *of* the discourse.

> Another index *of* the breadth *of* the dissemination *of* Christian literature *in* this period **is** the appearance *of* translations *of* Christian scriptural documents *into* a variety *of* provincial languages.

The *of* strings are the worst of all. They seem to reenact a series of hiccups. When you revise them, you can feel how fatally easy the "is" + prepositional-phrase Official Style formula is [!] for prose style. They blur the central action of the sentence—you can't tell what is actually going on. Let's try revising.

Original:
Here is an example *of* the use *of* the rule *of* justice *in* argumentation.

"Rule of justice" is a term of art, so we must leave it intact. After we have found an active verb—"exemplify"—buried in "is an example of the use of," the rest follows easily.

Revision:
This passage exemplifies argumentation using the rule of justice.

Now, how about the second sentence? It represents a perfectly symmetrical Official Style pattern: String of prepositional phrases + "is" + string of prepositional phrases. Let's diagram it for emphasis:

One

of the most important results
of the presentation
of the data

is the alteration

of the status
of the elements
of the discourse.

Notice the formulaic character? The monotonous rhythm? The blurred action? Try reading it aloud: *of* dadadum, *of* dadadum, *of* dadadum. I'm not sure what this sentence means, but the action must be buried in "alteration." Start there, with an active, transitive verb—"alter." How about "Presentation of the data alters the status of the discourse elements"? Or, less formally, "The status of the discourse elements depends on how you present the data." Or it may mean, "You don't know the status of the elements until you have presented the data." At least two different meanings swim beneath the formulaic prose. To revise it you must *rethink* it.

Now, the third sentence. Diagram first:

Another index
of the breadth

of the dissemination
of Christian literature
in this period

is the appearance

of translations
of Christian scriptural documents
into a variety
of provincial languages.

The standard Official Style sandwich: "is" between two thick layers of prepositional phrases. We know what to do: Generate an active, transitive verb, and get rid of those thick slices of prepositional phrases. Now, make no mistake about it; it is *hard* to figure out the central action in this sentence. Let me take a stab at it. First, we'll select an *actor.*

Translation of Christian scriptures into provincial languages . . .

Now, what is this "translation" *doing?*

shows how broadly Christian literature is disseminated. . . .

So how about this:

Translations into provincial languages show how broadly Christian scriptures were disseminated in this period.

It is not the greatest revision in the world, but we have cut the sentence length in half and reduced the prepositional phrases from eight to two. Often in revising an academic Official Style you discover, as here, that the root assertion is blurred and confused.

One more example of action-burial, this one in a shallow grave. A police report goes this way:

Subject officer attempted to enter his vehicle in order to report for work. He was confronted by a skunk who denied him entrance into his vehicle. An officer-involved shooting occurred, resulting in the demise of the skunk.

"An officer-involved shooting occurred, resulting in the demise of the skunk," instead of "He shot the skunk," shows the Official Style at its fullest and finest.

"BLAH BLAH *IS THAT*" OPENINGS

The formulaic slo-mo opening often provides your first taste of the Official Style. It delays and weakens the main action verb when (or *if*) you get to it. *The fact of the matter is that* we all fall into this habit. Let's look at some typical examples of what we will call the "Blah blah *is that*" opening from students, professors, and writers at large:

What I would like to signal here *is that* . . .

My contention *is that* . . .

What I want to make clear *is that* . . .

What has surprised me the most *is that* . . .

All that really means *is that* . . .

The upshot of what Heidegger says here *is that* . . .

The first *is that* . . .

The point I wish to make *is that* . . .

What I have argued here *is that* . . .

The important fundamental to remember *is that* . . .

My opinion *is that* on this point we have only two options . . .

My point *is that* the question of the discourse of the human sciences . . .

The fact of the matter *is that* the material of this article is drawn directly from . . .

Finally, the result of the use of all these new techniques and methods *is that* . . .

The one thing that Belinda does not realize *is that* Dorimant knows exactly how to press her buttons.

Easy to fix this pattern; just amputate the mindless preludial fan-fare. Start the sentence with whatever follows "Blah blah *is that....*" On a computer it couldn't be simpler: Do a global search for the phrase "is that" and revise it out each time it occurs.

> ~~The upshot of what~~ Heidegger says ~~here is~~ *that* ...
>
> ~~My opinion is that on this point~~ we have only two options ...
>
> ~~My point is that the question of~~ the discourse of the human sciences ...
>
> ~~The fact of the matter is that~~ the material of this article is drawn directly from ...

We can even improve my favorite from this anthology:

> ~~The one thing that~~ Belinda does not realize ~~is~~ that Dorimant knows exactly how to press her buttons.

By amputating the fanfare, you *start fast*, and a fast start may lead to major motion. That's what we're after. Where's the *action*?

Writers addicted to the "blah blah *is that*" dead-rocket opening often tie themselves in knots with it. One writes: "The position **we are at is this**." Another: "The traditional opposite notion **to this is that there are....**" And a third, a university professor, in an article accurately titled "On the Weakness of Language in the Human Sciences," offers this spasmodic set of **thises**, **thats**, and **whats**:

> Now **what** I would like to know specifically **is this**: **what is** the meaning of **this** "as" **that** Heidegger emphasizes so strongly when he says that **"that** which is explicitly understood"—**that is, that** which is interpreted—"has the structure of something as something"? My opinion **is that** what Heidegger means **is that** the structure of interpretation (*Auslegung*) is figural rather than, say, intentional. (My emphasis.)

In escaping from Houdini straightjackets like this, a couple of mechanical tricks come in handy. Besides eliminating the "is's" and changing every passive voice ("is defended by") to an active voice ("defends"), you can squeeze the compound verbs hard, make every "are able to" into a "can," every "seems to succeed in creating" into "creates," every "cognize the fact that" (no, I didn't make it up) into "think," every "am hopeful that" into "hope," every "provides us with an example of" into "exemplifies," every "seeks to reveal" into "shows," and every "there is the inclusion of" into "includes."

Then, after amputating those mindless *fact that* introductory-phrase fanfares, you'll start fast. After that fast start, get to the central action as soon as you can. Instead of "the answer is in the negative," you'll find yourself saying "No."

THE PM

We now have the beginnings of the Paramedic Method (PM):

1. Circle the prepositions.
2. Circle the "is" forms.
3. Find the *action*. Who's kicking who?
4. Put this action in a simple (not compound) active verb.
5. Start fast—no slow windups.

Let's use the PM on a more complex instance of blurred action, the opening sentences of an undergraduate psych paper:

> The history of Western psychological thought has long been dominated by philosophical considerations as to the nature of man. These notions have dictated corresponding considerations of the nature of the child within society, the practices by which children were to be raised, and the purposes of studying the child.

Two actions here—"dominate" and "dictate"—but neither has fully escaped from its native stone. The prepositional-phrase and infinitive strings just drag them down.

> The history
> *of* Western psychological thought . . .
> *by* philosophical considerations
> *as to* the nature
> *of* man . . .
> . . .

of the nature
of the child
within society . . .
by which children . . .
to be raised . . .
of studying . . .

In asking "Where's the action?," "Who's kicking who?," we next notice all the potential actions fermenting in the nouns: *thinking* in "thought," *consider* in "considerations," more *thinking* somewhere in "notions." They hint at actions they don't supply and so blur the actor-action relationship still further. We want, remember, a plain active verb, no prepositional-phrase strings, and a natural actor firmly in charge.

The **actor** must be: "philosophical considerations as to the nature of man."

The **verb:** "dominates."

The **object** of the action: "the history of Western psychological thought."

Now the real problems emerge. What does "philosophical considerations as to the nature of man" really mean? Buried down there is a question: "What is the nature of man?" The "philosophical considerations" just blur this question rather than narrow it. Likewise, the object of the action—"the history of Western psychological thought"—can be simply "Western psychological thought." Shall we put all this together in the passive form that the writer used?

Western psychological thought has been dominated by a single question: What is the nature of man?

Or, with an active verb:

A single question has dominated Western psychological thought: What is the nature of man?

Our formulaic concern with the stylistic surface—passives, prepositional phrases, kicker and kickee—has led to a much more focused thought.

The first sentence passes its baton awkwardly to the second. "Considerations," confusing enough as we have seen, become "these notions" at the beginning of the second sentence, and these "notions," synonymous with "considerations" in the first sentence, dictate more but different "considerations" in the second. We founder in these vague and vaguely synonymous abstractions. Our unforgiving eye for prepositional phrases then registers "*of* the nature *of* the child *within* society." We don't need "within society"; where else will psychology study children? And "the nature of the child" telescopes to "the child." We metamorphose "the practices by which children were to be raised" into "child-rearing," and "the purposes in studying the child" leads us back to "corresponding considerations of the nature of the child within society," which it partly overlaps. But we have now a definite actor, remember, in the first sentence—the "single question." So a tentative revision:

> This basic question leads to three others: What are children like? How should they be raised? Why should we study them?

Other revisions suggest themselves. Work out a couple. In mine, I've used "question" as the baton passed between the two sentences because it clarifies the relationship between the two. And I've tried to expose what real, clear action lies hidden beneath the conceptual cotton-wool of "these notions have dictated corresponding considerations."

Revision:
A single question has dominated Western psychological thought: What is the nature of man? This basic question leads to three others. What are children like? How should they be raised? Why should we study them?

A PAUSE FOR REFLECTION

This two-sentence example of student academic prose requires reflection. First, the sentences boast no grammatical or syntactical mistakes. Second, they need not have come from a student. Any

ACTION

issue of a psychology journal or text will net you a dozen from the same mold. How else did the student learn to write them? Third, few instructors reading this prose will think anything is wrong with it. Just the opposite. It reads just right; it sounds *professional*. The teacher's comment on this paper reads, in full: "An excellent paper—well conceived, well organized, and well written—A+." Yet a typical specimen sentence from it makes clear neither its main actor nor action; its thought consistently puffs into vague general concepts like "considerations" and "notions"; and its cradle-rocking monotonous rhythm puts us to sleep. It reveals a mind writing in formulas, out of focus, above all a mind putting no pressure on itself. The writer is not thinking so much as, on a scale slightly larger than normal, filling in the blanks. You can't build bridges thinking in this muddled way; they will fall down. If you bemuse yourself thus in a chemistry lab, you'll blow up the apparatus. And yet the student, obviously bright, has been invited to write this way and rewarded for it. He or she has been doing *a stylistic imitation*, and has brought if off successfully. Chances are that the focused, plain-language version I've offered would get a lower grade than the Official Style original. Revision is always perilous and paradoxical, but nowhere more so than in the academic world. Not so perilous, though, as bridges that fall down or lab apparatus that blows up. In the long run, it is better to get your thinking straight and take your chances.

When "is" Is OK

OK. We've been practicing the first five rules of the PM. Let's repeat them.

1. Circle the prepositions.
2. Circle the "is" forms.
3. Find the *action*. Who's kicking who?
4. Put this action in a simple (not compound) active verb.
5. Start fast—no slow windups.

At the center of this grouping stands the search for *action*. In the Official Style, action usually comes in only one flavor—"is." We've been revising "is" into transitive, active verbs that impart the breath of life.

But rules don't always work and exceptions exist, if not to disprove the rules, then to encourage common sense in applying them. To conclude this chapter, let's look at two passages that take an extreme stand toward "is." The first one uses nothing else. The second abjures it entirely.

First, a passage built on "is." It is from a famous military historian's discussion of the Battle of Agincourt.

> Agincourt is one of the most instantly and vividly visualized of all epic passages in English history, and one of the most satisfactory to contemplate. It is a victory of the weak over the strong, of the common soldier over the mounted knight, of resolution over bombast, of the desperate, cornered and far from home, over the proprietorial and cocksure. Visually it is a pre-Raphaelite, perhaps better a Medici Gallery print battle—a composition of strong verticals and horizontals and a conflict of rich dark reds and Lincoln greens against fishscale greys and arctic blues. . . . It is an episode to quicken the interest of any schoolboy ever bored by a history lesson, a set-piece demonstration of English moral superiority and cherished ingredient of a fading national myth. It is also a story of slaughter-yard behavior and of outright atrocity.

The passage is built on a backbone of "is." I've supplied the repetitions only implied by the text in **[boldface brackets]**.

Agincourt **is**
> one of the most instantly and vividly visualized of all epic passages in English history, and

> **[is]** one of the most satisfactory to contemplate.

It **is** a victory
> of the weak over the strong,

[It is a victory]
> of the common soldier over the mounted knight,

[It is a victory]
>of resolution over bombast,

[It is a victory]
>of the desperate, cornered and far from home, over the proprietorial and cocksure.

Visually it **is**
>a pre-Raphaelite, perhaps better a Medici Gallery print battle—a composition of strong verticals and horizontals and a conflict of rich dark reds and Lincoln greens against fishscale greys and arctic blues. . . .

It **is** an episode
>to quicken the interest of any schoolboy ever bored by a history lesson,

[It is]
>a set-piece demonstration of English moral superiority and cherished ingredient of a fading national myth.

It **is** also
>a story of slaughter-yard behavior and of outright atrocity.

Goodness! Everything I've been preaching against! "Is" plus strings of prepositional phrases. But the prose works in this instance because it possesses a shape, a repetitive, chorus-like pattern of similar elements until, in the last sentence, the prose shape remains the same but the sense constitutes a 180-degree inverted climax. Sentence shape matters. Shape attracts our attention and our exploration of the Official Style must consider how such attraction works.

Now for the opposite extreme, an excerpt from an article from the field of artificial intelligence which makes its point by banishing "to be" completely.

>To devise a new kind of logic we must escape from the old metaphysics. I shall indicate how I have tried to do this. One valuable technique which I recommend, I shall apply in writing this essay. I shall endeavor to write this essay without using the verb "to be." By doing so, I shall subject myself, in an informal way, to an essential discipline which a logic of action should impose, formally, upon its users. This discipline

forces one to think in terms of actions and agents and deprives one of that easy way of begging epistemological questions—the impersonal assertion of truth or existence in the style we normally expect of scientific writers.

We've been illustrating just this "essential discipline," the need to build upon a central action. But, as these two examples show, you can do so in different ways.

2

Attention

Revising Prose practices sentence-level revision. If you can see how an individual sentence works, you can scale that knowledge up to paragraph and beyond. In this chapter, we'll try thinking about the individual sentence in a new way—as an economy, an economy in miniature. Economics, according to the usual definition, studies "the allocation of scarce resources which have alternative uses." You might think that, in writing, *ideas* are the commodity in short supply. Most people would agree with you. But when you are revising, the scarcest resource is human attention. Sentences are attention economies. Ideas have to get your attention before you will pay attention to them. And, as we all know, the alternative uses for human attention multiply by the day. Some economists argue that in our information economy, attention is now the scarcest resource. This shift makes sentence economics more important than ever. It brings prose revision into alignment with our thinking about human effort on a larger scale.

Here's a chunk—it is so lifeless you want to use a word like "chunk" or "lump" or "heap"—of typical Official Style prose.

> What are the behavioral factors that induce employees to load up on company stock? One factor is people's tendency to be overconfident and excessively optimistic. Another behavioral factor deserving attention is inertia.

How does this lump allocate its scarce commodity, the reader's attention? First sentence first.

> What are the behavioral factors that induce employees to load up on company stock?

"Behavioral factors"? What are these? Not clear. You must stop and think. Are "behavioral factors" any different from plain "behavior"? Are they just ordinary "motives," the reasons we invest in Plan A rather than Plan B? No way to tell, but we've spent some precious scarce attention trying to decide. The problem with "What are the behavioral factors that induce . . ." is not simply wordiness, that all-purpose term of abuse. The problem is *waste*, waste of attention on a simple question: "Why do employees . . . ?" We've squandered our precious resource. But wait. As sometimes happens, this sentence changes stylistic register in midsentence. The writer lapses into ordinary comprehensible prose: "load up on company stock." We need only glue the two parts of the sentence back together:

> Why do employees load up on company stock?

Now we have a plain question that asks for a plain answer. On we go to the second sentence.

> One factor is people's tendency to be overconfident and excessively optimistic.

The answer we seek lies in "overconfident" and "excessively optimistic." But look at how long it takes to get there and the distractions placed along the way: "factor"—well, I wonder exactly what that means? And "tendency"? Are they overconfident or are they not? We have a question: "Why do employees load up on company stock?" How can we answer it most economically? Easy. "Why do employees load up on company stock? Overconfidence and overoptimism." But what about "Another behavioral factor deserving attention is inertia"? Problem: The vital ingredient, the target for the reader's attention, is "inertia" and it comes last, after wasting more of our attention. Answer: Just add it to our answer list and skip the rest.

Why do employees load up on company stock? Overconfidence, overoptimism, and inertia.

But wait a final minute. Do we need "overconfidence" *and* "overoptimism"? Doesn't "overconfidence" cover both? It seems to, and so we have this as a final revision:

Why do employees load up on company stock? Overconfidence and inertia.

Finally, a shape and rhythm that, by focusing our attention, reinforce the argument. An excess—overconfidence—balanced by a deficiency—inertia. The ideas balance and so does the shape of the sentence. "Why X? Y and Z."

This passage was written by economists about investment. How would they rate an investment that wastes two thirds of its investable assets? That's what's happened here: 11 words instead of 32, lard factor (LF) 66%.

TRANSFER OF POWER

Why has there been no transfer here of economic thinking to economic prose? Why no transfer of power from argument to expression? Why do these writers, who study the efficient allocation of scarce resources, waste two thirds of their vital resource—the reader's attention? Precious little of such transfer occurs in any field. Here, for example, is a sentence from, of all things, a writing textbook.

One of the factors that limits and warps the development of a theory of composition and style by teachers of the subject is the tendency to start with failed or inadequate writing and to project goodness as the opposite of badness.

Nothing in the sentence draws your attention to the structural logic of the sentence: actor, action, object. Possible actors there are aplenty:

factors
development
theory

composition
style
teachers
subject

And incipient actions too:

limiting
warping
developing
tending
starting
failing
projecting

But nothing in the sentence's *shape* narrows down our attention among the cornucopia of possible actors and actions. So let's apply the PM for a start.

> One **of** the factors that limits and warps the development **of** a theory **of** composition and style **by** teachers **of** the subject *is* the tendency *to* start **with** failed or inadequate writing and *to* project goodness as the opposite **of** badness.

This writing teacher has left the choice of subject up to us. I guess that *teachers* are the primary actor. So we can proceed with "Composition teachers. . . ." What are they *doing*? They are *starting*. So a step further gives us "Composition teachers often start. . . ." What are they starting with? "bad writing." So, step three, "Composition teachers often start with bad writing and define good writing as the opposite." That's one assertion. Now for the second, the "theory" part. Hard to see how to revise it, because the sentence yokes two different assertions but does not make clear their relationship. My try: "You can't develop a negative theory of composition." Maybe you can do better. Try it.

Here's the original again.

> One of the factors that limits and warps the development of a theory of composition and style by teachers of the subject is the tendency to

start with failed or inadequate writing and to project goodness as the opposite of badness. (41 words)

And the revision thus far:

Composition teachers often start with bad writing and define good writing as the opposite. But you can't develop a negative theory of composition. (23 words)

A LF of 44%. But that percentage does not fully explain how our scarce resource—our attention—is wasted. That comes with all those incipient actors and actions that are suggested. You don't need "limits and warps": One will do. You don't need "composition and style": One will do. You don't need "failed or inadequate": Failed writing is inadequate. And if you say "often" you don't need a "factor" which turns into a "tendency." What's going on? The writer cannot make up her or his mind and unloads the task on us. We must spend the time the writer has saved by not deciding on a single apt word; the writer's cost has been unloaded on us. Back to the efficient allocation of scarce resources that have alternative uses. A single writer saves time by not thinking an argument through; the many readers must each spend the time so saved. If a writer spends the time to get the sentence right, all the readers profit. That may be what "profit" in a sentence means. The readers profit from a previous expenditure by the writer. Not here. And the writer is a *writing teacher*!

(Time out for a "full disclosure" on this example. Its argument rubs me the wrong way. The passage warns us against doing just what I have done to the passage: Start with lumpen prose and try to make it better. If you don't revise, you'll end up writing prose like this, warning us that prose revision is a bad idea.)

Here's a third example, this time from an outfit whose business is the economics of attention. Again, no transfer of power from the argument to the expression.

University Communications increases awareness, understanding and support of U of C's vision, mission, and accomplishments among its many constituencies. A major focus of this division is the formulation and implementation of strategic communications initiatives and plans that support a desired image and sets of perceptions of U of C. This division maintains the University's home page and publishes *U of C Magazine* and *U of C Today* (faculty/staff newspaper), in addition to coordinating media and public relations functions for the academic and administrative leadership of the campus.

This is the university public relations staff talking. They are attention economists; their job is to catch this public's attention and direct it. Here's how they begin.

University Communications increases awareness, understanding, and support of U of C's vision, mission, and accomplishments among its many constituencies.

Let's praise something for a change, an attempt to create a shape within the sentence by the triple parallelisms: awareness, understanding, support/vision, mission, accomplishments. But the weight of all those nouns swamps the lame verb: "increases." And they are all vague. Try keeping in mind, in a single mental frame, awareness, understanding, support, vision, mission, accomplishments. You can't. Your attention is not focused but blurred.

Next, a perfectly typical Official Style sentence:

A major focus of this division is the formulation and implementation of strategic communications initiatives and plans that support a desired image and sets of perceptions of U of C.

It's a parade of buzzwords: focus, formulation, implementation, strategic (the buzziest word going), initiatives. And a sentence shape utterly without the "focus" that constitutes any PR outfit's main job.

A major focus
of this division
is
the formulation
and implementation
of strategic communications initiatives

and plans
that support
a desired image
and sets
of perceptions
of U of C.

Dadada, dadada, is, dadada . . . of . . . and . . . of . . . of . . . . No
rhythm, no evidence of energy, blood flow, human life. And look
at the "shun" words: division, formulation, implementation, communications, perceptions. The whole passage is full of long, jaw-
breaking Latinate nouns, bricks that build a wall of boredom the
reader runs smack into. Remember, these people are in the business of allocating a scarce resource—human attention. You don't
do that by making the reader run into a brick wall.

Next sentence in this disastrous revelation of PR incompetence:

> This division maintains the University's home page and publishes *U of
> C Magazine* and *U of C Today* (faculty/staff newspaper) . . .

Ah! Finally something specific, concrete. Nothing wrong with this
sentence so far that a little rhythmic adjustment won't fix:

> This division maintains the University's home page and publishes *U of
> C Magazine* and the faculty/staff newspaper *U of C Today* . . .

A newspaper is something ~~concrete~~—we don't want to downgrade
it to a parenthesis. And this way, *U of C Today*, because it now
comes at the end of the sentence, gets a little more stress. In the
midst of all the hot air about "formulation and implementation of
strategic communications initiatives," we need a concrete product.

Now for the rest of the sentence.

> . . . in addition to coordinating media and public relations functions
> [relation*shuns*, func*shuns*—don't these attention economists *have*
> *ears*?] for the academic and administrative leadership of the campus.

At last we have come to what this office does—*public relations*. It is
shunted into a subordinate position, of course, and surrounded by

a protective membrane of *shun* words. But that is what this office *does*—public relations. Let's essay a revision starting with that.

> University Communications handles public relations for the university. We create the University's public image. We tell our friends what we are doing and hope to do, and why, and ask for their support to do it. We do this by maintaining the University's home page and by publishing its alumni magazine, *U of C Magazine*, and our faculty and staff newspaper, *U of C Today.*

We've reduced the passage by 25%, but that reduction comes from making a much bigger change. Ask yourself, does the revision omit anything essential in the original? When you "increase awareness, understanding and support of U of C's vision, mission, and accomplishments among its many constituencies," aren't you telling your friends what the university is doing and hopes to do? Doesn't "a major focus of this division is the formulation and implementation of strategic communications initiatives and plans" amount to conducting the university's public relations? And doesn't "support a desired image and sets of perceptions" mean "creating our public image"?

But the revision does leave out a lot. It omits the vital message. The original, ostensibly written for the general public, really addresses the university bureaucracy. It seeks to show how important the division is, how many miraculous tasks it performs, how much larger its budget should be to do them—sorry, to facilitate their implementation—as they should be done. But worse than omitting these vital messages, the revision reveals what the whole passage exists to hide: that the division is ashamed of what it does. Public relations people are economists of attention. They specialize in allocating human attention. Their job is to create a public face for the university that will attract the right kind of attention and a lot of money. But this message, while leaking out in a phrase like "a desired image," can't be said in plain language. The Official Style's rich repertoire of euphemism comes to the rescue. We can say it without saying it. Since our bureaucratic audience isn't really competing for anybody's attention, it need not worry about speaking plainly, about cutting to the chase. The bureaucracy supplies a monopolistic audience of guaranteed mutual boredom. Can you imagine using this kind of prose as a pitch to snare a public relations campaign in the marketplace?

In each of the three passages we've just examined, the writers have not applied their professional talents to their prose. There has been no transfer of power from argument to expression. For that transfer to occur, writers have to look AT their prose rather than simply THROUGH it, apply their talents to their discourse. Revision teaches you how to do this.

ATTENTION COSTS

Now here's an example where a transfer of power has occurred. The management talents and attitudes needed to run a company have infused the prose. Nucor Corporation has been described as "the most entrepreneurial and innovative steelmaker in the world." It has led in delegated authority and flattened hierarchy as well. As its president, John Correnti, has said: "When we were a $1 billion company we had 18 people in our corporate headquarters. When we were a $1.5 billion company we had 19. . . . I'll fight at all costs to avoid building up a corporate hierarchy. It stifles growth, it stifles ingenuity, and it stifles that entrepreneurial spirit."[1]

Here's how Correnti describes his philosophy of management:

I can't melt steel or roll steel or sell steel or account for steel as well as those guys in that plant who do that for a living. A lot of people think that because they have the title president or executive vice president, they know more about the business than the guys on the shop floor and that's not true. I know more about the general part of it than they do, but the melter knows more about melting steel than I do, the roller knows more about rolling steel, and the sales people know more about selling steel. So you give them the encouragement to do their jobs to the best of their ability and you push it downward.[2]

---

[1]Quoted in *The Renaissance of American Steel*, Roger S. Ahlbrandt, Richard J. Fruehan, and Frank Giarratani (New York: Oxford University Press, 1996), pp. 43, 70.

[2]*Renaissance of American Steel*, p. 65.

Notice *the way he says it?* A believable, direct, real voice. The company is not bureaucratic and the style is not Official. He did not say:

> In the operation of our manufacturing facilities, it has been decided that those individuals occupying senior positions should not engage in micromanagement situations which result in the usurpation of melting functions from those individuals actually engaged in the process of the melting of the steel in the facilities of the Corporation. (etc.)

Correnti's prose gets actor and action together in the same way his management philosophy does. The shape of his description follows the shape of the business: making steel, selling it, keeping track of the sales. See the natural shape?

I can't	melt steel
	or	roll steel
	or	sell steel
	or	account for steel

as well as those guys in that plant who do that for a living.

A lot of	people think that
because	they have the title president or executive vice president,
	they know more about the business than the guys on the shop floor

and that's not true.

I know more about the general part of it than they do,

but	the melter knows more about melting steel than I do,
	the roller knows more about rolling steel,
and	the sales people know more about selling steel.

So you give them the encouragement to do their jobs to the best of their ability and you push it downward.

Prose like this can be spoken. *It has a voice.* The Official Style cannot speak; it can only float down from above in hierarchical layers. It is the "voice" of remote hierarchy. As such, it grates against the entrepreneurial temper of the time. Entrepreneurial prose wants to get going—no slow windups. The Official Style wants to freeze the action. A believable voice *gets your attention*. So do the shape and rhythm of this passage. Power has been transferred from the argument to its expression. We perceive the world through shapes and we enjoy it through rhythms. Correnti uses both here to construct a voice you enjoy listening to. Try reading the passage aloud; not mumbling your way through it, mind, but with vigor and emphasis.

Now try reading this passage the same way. The subject is the same: *implementation*, to use the buzzword, or more simply, getting something done.

> A proposed planning process for implementation of this initiative is attached. Emphasizing transparency, this process is targeting an implementation plan by Summer 2005.

The voice of inertia, imprisoned in a terminology. Is "a proposed planning process" anything more than a "plan"? The Official Style, as we have seen, likes to add "process" or "situation" to anything to make it sound more ponderous and official. "Termination" turns into "the termination process." "Inventory" into "the inventorying process." In this passage, doesn't a "plan" imply planning? And isn't "proposed" implied by a plan? What else could a plan do but propose an action? "Implement" as a verb means "to carry into effect" according to *Webster's New World Dictionary*, and an "initiative" means "taking the first step or move." So, stacking up the *actions* in this first sentence looks like this: We are *proposing* to start a *process* to *plan* to *carry into effect a taking of the first step*. Imagine putting someone who thinks this way in charge of pouring steel!

"Emphasizing transparency" is simply a buzzword filler. So we are back to "process," which, as we have seen, means "plan." This plan is "targeting an implementation plan." A plan targeting a plan? "Implementation," we now know, means "to carry into effect." So the plan is targeting a plan to carry into effect a plan. Next summer.

What does it all mean? My guess: "We plan to make these changes by next summer." From 23 words to 9. LF 61%. But the real waste comes in the lack of "transparency," which, ironically enough, it says will be emphasized. The more you ponder these two sentences, the more opaque and nonsensical they become.

The Toyota system of industrial production has a word for this: *muda*. Waste. Attention puzzles like these sell their message at a high cost—*attention muda*. Only bureaucracies, which move at a snail's pace—if you're lucky—can afford them.

Winston Churchill knew this in August 1940, at the height of the German invasion scare. He begged his subordinates to be less long-winded.

> I ask my colleagues and their staffs to see to it that their Reports are shorter. . . . Let us have an end of such phrases as these: "It is also of importance to bear in the mind the following considerations . . ." or "Consideration should be given to the possibility of carrying into effect. . . ." Most of these woolly phrases are mere padding, which can be left out altogether, or replaced by a single word. **Let us not shrink from using the short expressive phrase, even if it is conversational.** [My emphasis.][3]

Churchill had to animate a lethargic bureaucracy, and economizing on communication costs seemed a good way to, well, initiate the implementation of the animation process.

Imagine what Churchill might have said about the "proposed planning process" passage (sorry, but it asks for a comic "p" alliteration). For its problems run deeper. The writer thinks that something comprehensible has been said, instead of tautological nonsense. She has fooled *herself.* And she labors under a worse illusion, that communication has occurred when it has not, that the reader gets the message, too.

"It's Nothing Serious"

Here is a good place to confront a common response to revision pressures like this. "Oh, it's nothing serious. People read that guff all day long. They're used to it. They just skim through the buzzwords. They get the message." Trouble is, mostly they don't. If you write nonsense and don't know it, and people read it and don't see

---

[3]War Cabinet Paper No. 211 of 1940, "Brevity." *The Churchill War Papers* (W. W. Norton, New York, 1995), v. 2, p. 636.

that it is nonsense—that you are processing a plan to target a plan to begin a plan—then you've tacitly agreed to share a muddled illusion. If real action is needed, the muddle can become expensive.

The buzzwords that lard such shared illusions—facility, area, factor, model, strategy, input—shift the cost of communication, and thus of thinking, from the writer to the reader. And the cost is high because a single writer's ineptitude is paid for by many readers. These buzzwords create a tacit agreement on both sides to stop thinking, settle for a vague, high level of generality. They translate specific information into its nearest bureaucratic generalized equivalent. A word like "facility" drains the immediacy out of life: a "plant," a "warehouse," a "store," a "prison," all bleach into a colorless generalized "facility." Then, of course, you need an adjective to specify what you have just generalized: manufacturing facility, storage facility, incarceration facility. You have renounced the language's rich store of words, thrown away a priceless asset, and then tried to control the damage. *Attention muda.*

At the center of this tacit agreement that nonsense makes sense lurks (I use "lurks" advisedly, since tacit agreements shun conscious recognition) the assumption that style "doesn't matter," only ideas do. We'll return to this argument later, but here we might put it directly in the context of an attention economy. The package doesn't matter, only the contents do. But in an attention economy, the brand is vital. Companies manage their brands as their central assets. In an attention economy, style matters. That means that prose style matters. Shape and rhythm are not just ornaments. They are vital assets in gaining a reader's attention. And sooner or later, neglecting them will come home to you. Nonsense will be seen as what it is—wasteful and dangerous.

A PAUSE FOR REFLECTION

Our Paramedic Method now has six steps:

1. Circle the prepositions.
2. Circle the "is" forms.
3. Find the *action.*

4. Put this action in a simple active verb.
5. Start fast—no slow windups.
6. Read the passage aloud with emphasis and feeling.

Using the Paramedic Method takes time. Yes, of course it does. PM revision takes hard work, too. These are costs a writer must bear. But that hard necessity only reveals the magnitude of the problem. We are talking about big mistakes not fine details. A recent police sting in Silicon Valley recovered a horde of stolen computer chips. The police officer who spoke to the press wanted to point out that they had seen only the tip of the iceberg, the froth on the latte, the surface of the lake. So he said "What you see here? It amounts to comparably nothing." Huh? Something? Nothing? Huh? So with the examples we have worked through in this chapter. They point to a gigantic problem, a massive failure to employ the machinery of intellection. A huge waste of time and thought. *Muda.* Eliminating prose *muda* may be, to think for a moment like an economist, the last unexplored competitive advantage. It all starts with the single sentence. Learning that buzzwords create only buzz; getting your mind straight before you open your mouth or pick up your pen; fixing actor, action, and result in your mind, all these take you into the heart of an attention economy.

We are, then, considering serious matters. Here's an example of how serious. When asked about whether the piece of foam had damaged the Space Shuttle which later killed the crew, a member of the Mission Management Team remarked:

> And I really don't think there is much we can do so it is really not a factor during the flight because there is not much we can do about it.

Was she really thinking about what she was saying? The problem here is not Official Style obfuscation; a bureaucrat is taking evasive action without really thinking about what such action means. We can't do anything about it, so we choose not to think about it. But there was, at least according to some commentators, something that could have been done about it, had NASA chosen to pay attention to it. If the Mission Management Team had listened to what it was saying. But it wasn't. Style, they might have said, doesn't matter. But it did.

CHAPTER

3

Voice

Like the elements of an economy, the elements of prose style— grammar, syntax, shape, rhythm, emphasis, level, usage—all work as dependent variables. Change one and you change the rest. Rhythm and sound seem, for most prose writers, the most dependent of all. They affect nothing and everything affects them. They do affect something, though. They affect *us*. Rhythm constitutes the most vital of prose's vital life signs. Rhythmless, unemphatic prose always indicates that something has gone wrong.

TIN EARS

Tin ears, insensitivity to the sound of words, indicate that the hearing that registers rhythm has been turned off. Tin ears have become so common that often you can't tell mistakes from mindlessness. Was this sentence written tongue in cheek or only wax in ears?

> Conflict, chaos, competition and combat combine to constitute both the labor and fertilizer of war and the fruit of this is honor.

Too resolute an alliteration, too many "c" sounds.

> <u>C</u>onflict, <u>c</u>haos, <u>c</u>ompetition and <u>c</u>ombat <u>c</u>ombine to <u>c</u>onstitute both the labor and fertilizer of war and the fruit of this is honor.

"Fertilizer" and "fruit" doesn't help, either. "Conflict" is a near synonym for "combat" and overlaps with "competition"; and if you use "constitute" you don't need "combine." Nor does "this" refer to anything specific. Yet the sentence conceals a rhythm waiting for liberation. A little subtle subtraction leads to this:

> Combat, competition, and chaos constitute the fertilizer of war and the fruit of this fertilizer is honor.

Since "constitute the fertilizer of" = "fertilize," one further change yields a sentence with a sound and shape of its own:

> Combat, competition, and chaos fertilize war and produce its fruit—honor. (LF 50%)

We've kept the alliterative yoking of the opening triplet phrase and created a rhythmically emphatic place of honor for—*honor.*

The Official Style, deaf and blind, creates rhythm and shape only by accident. So, for example, a U.S. government attorney refuses to talk about a controversial spy case with commendable, if desperate, pertinacity:

> I can't comment. We will not comment. We are not going to comment.

This three-segment climax has been used since classical times (when it was called *tricolon crescens,* each of the three elements being slightly longer than the previous one, thus building to a climax) as part of a sentence strategy for building long rhythmic periodic sentences. (I define and illustrate "periodic sentence" later in this chapter.) Winston Churchill was especially fond of it:

> Victory at all costs, victory in spite of all terror, victory however long and hard the road may be. . . .

> This is not the end. It is not even the beginning of the end. But it is, perhaps, the end of the beginning.

VOICE

The Official Style creates tin ears, and when the ear atrophies, any hope of colloquial emphasis or climax fades away. But when there is a voice to begin with, things are much easier to fix. Look at this flawed diamond:

> There is not a sign of life in the whole damned paper (with the possible exception of line 72).

A cinch to fix. Reverse the order and be generous about line 72:

> Except for line 72, there is not a sign of life in the whole damn paper.

Terrific!

CHANGE-UPS

Sometimes you can notice a colloquial voice change abruptly to an Official Style one: "This point just emphasizes the need of repeated experience for properly utilizing the various sense modalities." The sentence breaks in half after "experience." We expect a finish like, "to use all the senses," and get instead an Official Style translation. Here is a scholar doing the same thing, this time from sentence to sentence:

[Official Style]

> The establishment of an error detection mechanism is necessary to establish a sense of independence in our own movement planning and correction.

[Change-up to Plain English]

> Unless we know we are doing something wrong, we can't correct it.

Change-ups like this emphasize the voicelessness of the Official Style.

Voice usually gets squeezed out of student prose by the Official Style. So we should celebrate an exception, a geography paper with real ears:

> Twice daily, at sunrise and sunset, a noisy, smokeridden train charges into the stillness of the Arabian desert. Winding about the everchanging windblown sand dunes, the "Denver Zephyr" not only defies the fatal forces of the notorious deserts, but for the nonnative, offers an extraordinary encounter with the tightly closed Saudi society.

The "s" assonance—sunrise, sunset, noisy, smokeridden, stillness—works, and so does "fatal forces"; and "**forces**" echoes part of "not**orious**," which, with "deserts," defines those forces. The sentence allows the voice a full tonal range, a chance for pitch to rise and fall, and a chance to build a climax on "tightly closed Saudi society" as well. This expanded tonal range, alas, went unappreciated by the tin-eared Official Style instructor: The paper was marked down for being too "journalistic." No good deed goes unpunished.

I'm suggesting that writers should become self-conscious about the sound of words. Once our ears have had their consciousness raised, they'll catch the easy problems as they flow from the pen—"however clever" will become "however shrewd" in the first draft—and the harder ones will seem easier to revise.

ARRHYTHMIA ATTACKS

Now for some arrhythmia attacks from a batch of undergraduate papers. The first illustrates the power of a single verb—or lack of one.

> Reputation is also a serious consideration for native Trojans.

Why not:

> Trojans worship reputation. (LF 66%)

The Official Style lends the following sentence an unintended lubricious suggestion:

> The first duty of female characters in the drama of this period is to illustrate the various dimensions of the male protagonist.

Why not:

> In drama of this period female characters must above all illuminate the male protagonist. (LF 36%)

And how about

> Both film and song ask the eternal questions of young adulthood.

as a revision of

> A good measure of this appeal can be traced to the fact that both the visual medium of the film and aural medium of the song confront the young person with eternal questions of young adulthood.

The revision, by keeping the sentence short, preserves the natural ending emphasis for "young adulthood," and so gives the voice someplace to go. And you can't beat a LF of 69%. Try reading both aloud several times. See what I mean?

It is not only student prose that has lost its voice but business writing as well. Here a businessman tells us about his firm's new health plan:

> When the sorting of the various problems was taking place, additional vitamins were introduced, cocktails reduced to a minimum, and a regular exercise program begun.

A natural *tricolon crescens* springs forth:

> While the plan was starting up, we took vitamins, laid off the booze, and began a regular exercise program.

Consider now two longer examples of contrasting prose voices. The first comes from a bureaucrat at the Michigan Department of Environmental Quality. In the second, the target of the bureaucrat's threat replies. First the threat:

> It has come to the attention of the Department of Environmental Quality that there has been recent unauthorized activity on the above referenced parcel of property. You have been certified as the legal landowner and/or contractor who did the following unauthorized activity: Construction and maintenance of two wood debris dams across the outlet stream of Spring Pond. A permit must be issued prior to the start of this type of activity. . . . The Department has been informed that one or both of the dams partially failed during a recent rain event, causing debris dams and flooding at downstream locations. We find that dams of this nature are inherently hazardous and cannot be permitted. . . . Failure to comply with this request, or any further unauthorized activity on the site, may result in this case being referred for elevated enforcement action. . . .

The authentic Official Style: Land becomes a "parcel of property," "rain" becomes a "rain event," and the threat of a fine turns into "elevated enforcement action." Passives, prepositional-phrase trains, the full monty. But note the *voice*—the genuine niggling mindlessness of a bureaucrat on autopilot.

The perpetrator of this "unauthorized activity on the site" replied:

> A couple of beavers are in the (state unauthorized) process of constructing and maintaining two wood "debris" dams across the outlet stream of my Spring Pond. While I did not pay for, nor authorize, their dam project, I think they would be highly offended that you call their skillful use of natural building materials "debris." . . . As to your dam request [that] the beavers first must fill out a dam permit prior to the start of this type of dam activity, my first dam question to you is: are you trying to discriminate against my Spring Pond Beavers or do you require all dam beavers throughout this State to conform to said dam request? If you are not discriminating against these particular beavers, please send me completed copies of all those other applicable beaver dam permits. . . . I seriously hope you are not selectively enforcing

this dam policy—or once again both I and the Spring Pond Beavers will scream prejudice![1]

The voice of common sense, but sensible enough to clothe itself in the insane logic of the bureaucracy.

THE PARAMEDIC METHOD—FULL FORM

Often, when dealing with the Official Style, we must try revising a passage even if we are not sure what it means. In these cases, we may begin to understand the special terms by trying to fathom their relationship. Practice such a "naive analysis," a "revise-to-understand exercise" on the following wonderfully arrhythmic sentence from a book about rhythm!

Rhythm is that property of a sequence of events in time which produces in the mind of the observer the impression of proportion between the directions of the several events or groups of events of which the sequence is composed.

Look at what the prepositional-phrase strings do to the rhythm of this passage about rhythm:

Rhythm **is** that property
of a sequence
of events
in time
    which produces
in the mind
of the observer the impression
of proportion
between the directions
of the several events or groups
of events
of which the sequence is composed.

---

[1] *Wall Street Journal*, 3/30/98. The article concludes: "The Michigan Department of Environmental Quality informs us that the case has been closed."

Can we revise in a way to show that the writer has mastered his subject as well as written about it? Try it, using the full form of the Paramedic Method to help. (See my best try in the addendum to this chapter.)

1. Circle the prepositions.
2. Circle the "is" forms.
3. Find the *action*.
4. Put this action in a simple (not compound) active verb.
5. Start fast—no slow windups.
6. Read the passage aloud with emphasis and feeling.
7. Write out each sentence on a blank screen or sheet of paper and mark off its basic rhythmic units with a "/".
8. Mark off sentence length with a "/".

If you are trying to alert yourself to voice, sentence length is one of the easiest PM tests to apply. Take a piece of your prose and a red pencil and draw a slash after every sentence. Two or three pages ought to make a large enough sample. If the red marks occur at regular intervals, you have, as they used to say in the Nixon White House, a problem. You can chart the problem another way, if you like. Choose a standard length for one sentence and then do a bar graph. If it looks like this,

dandy. If like this,

not so dandy. Obviously, no absolute quantitative standards exist for how much variety is good, how little bad, but the principle couldn't be easier. Vary your sentence lengths. Give your voice a chance to change pitch and timbre. Naturally enough, complex patterns will fall into long sentences and emphatic conclusions work well when short. But no inviolable rule prevails except avoid monotony.

A LIVING VOICE

The following passage obeys this inviolable rule. It comes from a brilliantly written World War II memoir by Brendan Phibbs, *The Other Side of Time*. Phibbs has been talking about the self-dramatizing, self-serving American General George Patton, and moves from there to Patton's mirror opposite, General Lucien Truscott:

> And now, we said more happily, consider ... Truscott. ... Men like this are stamped, early in life, and the outlines of the mold spell honesty. They fill the mold without effort; it fits them and they have no question about who they are and what they can do. They're free of the need to grimace and prance; they're free to spend themselves on a cause, for an ideal, scorning advantage and chaining the ego in some remote corner to babble and shriek and rattle its shackles. Having won, they're satisfied with the achievement; they're not driven to seek their value in the gaze and the wonder of others, and they walk off into the quiet corners of history where the truth lives, grinning to watch impostors scribbling their worthless names across the walls of the public baths.

The quiet corners of history where the truth lives—what a wonderful phrase. What creates the rhythm? The sense of authentic voice? Of sentences with a shape that energizes meaning? Well, we might start by graphing them. Graphing is much easier when you write on an electronic screen; simple and cheap graphing programs lie ready to hand:

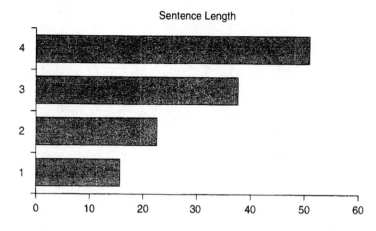

Sentence Length

A varied, climactic sentence length. But that only begins to describe how it works. Let's apply Rule 7 and mark off basic rhythmic units.

> And now, we said more happily, consider...Truscott. / . . . Men like this are stamped, / early in life, / and the outlines of the mold spell / honesty. / They fill the mold without effort; / it fits them / and they have no question about who they are / and what they can do. / They're free of the need to grimace and prance; / they're free to spend themselves on a cause, / for an ideal, /scorning advantage / and chaining the ego / in some remote corner / to babble and shriek and rattle its shackles. / Having won, / they're satisfied with the achievement; / they're not driven to seek their value in the gaze and the wonder of others, / and they walk off into the quiet corners of history where the truth lives, / grinning to watch impostors scribbling their worthless names / across the walls of the public baths.

What do the rhythmic units look like when diagrammed?

> Men like this are stamped, /
> early in life, /
> and the outlines of the mold spell /

honesty. /
They fill the mold without effort; /
it fits them /
and they have no question about who they are /
and what they can do. /
They're free of the need to grimace and prance; /
they're free to spend themselves on a cause, /
for an ideal, /
scorning advantage /
and chaining the ego /
in some remote corner /
to babble and shriek and rattle its shackles. /
Having won, /
they're satisfied with the achievement; /
they're not driven to seek their value in the gaze and the wonder of
others, /
and they walk off into the quiet corners of history where the truth
lives, /
grinning to watch impostors scribbling their worthless names /
across the walls of the public baths.

I don't claim this division is linguistically correct, whatever
that might mean. Just the opposite. It is a quick and easy
method any of us can use to chart our own reading of a passage
to imagine how our voice might embody the prose rhythm.
Charting makes us specify, *become self-conscious about*, our own
rhythmic interpretation. There's no better way to spot how sentence rhythm and shape work than to use Rules 6–8 of the PM.
Again:

6. Read the passage aloud with emphasis and feeling.
7. Write out each sentence on a blank screen or sheet of
   paper and mark off its basic rhythmic units with a "/".
8. Mark off sentence length with a "/".

What have they told us for this passage? Well, that the basic
rhythmic units, at least as I hear them, vary markedly in length.

Second, that the passage invites stress on a series of crucial words. Again, let me show you what I mean:

Men like this are stamped, /
early in life, /
and the outlines of the mold spell /
honesty. /
They fill the mold without effort; /
it fits them /
and they have no question about who they are /
and what they can do. /
They're free of the need to grimace and prance; /
they're free to spend themselves on a cause, /
for an ideal, /
scorning advantage /
and chaining the ego /
in some remote corner /
to babble and shriek and rattle its shackles. /
Having won, /
they're satisfied with the achievement; /
they're not driven to seek their value in the gaze and the wonder of others, /
and they walk off into **the quiet corners of history where the truth lives,** /
grinning to watch impostors scribbling their worthless names /
across the walls of the public baths.

The PM lends itself naturally to the typographic expressivity of an electronic screen. The two work together to give anyone who cares about prose the power to analyze how a passage works. The simple typographical diagram I've just invented immediately sensitizes us to the passage's voice and rhythm. It builds toward a definite climax in a memorable phrase, sets up a strong emphasis on **honesty,** and develops from that a meditation that ends up being about **the quiet corners of history where the truth lives.** And notice how many strong verb forms, how many actions, the passage contains?

Stamped
Spell honesty
Fill the mold
What they can *do*
grimace and *prance*
spend themselves on a cause
chaining the ego
babble and *shriek* and *rattle* its shackles
Having *won*
driven to *seek*
walk off into the quiet corners
grinning to *watch* impostors
scribbling their worthless names

The passage recreates for us how history is both acted and reenacted, how it happens and how we seek its truth, waiting there for us in quiet corners. Phibbs wants to describe how we respond to social situations, how we elicit *from* them what we bring *to* them.

A DEAD VOICE

Now, for contrast, here is a passage of genuinely awesome arrhythmic unintelligibility from an American sociologist. It talks about, as the editor explains—as far as I can understand him, much less the sociologist—the background expectancies of situations that make social interaction possible. That is to say, it covers—I think—much the same ground as the Phibbs passage.

The properties of indexical expressions and indexical actions are ordered properties. These consist of organizationally demonstrable sense, or facticity, or methodic use, or agreement among "cultural colleagues." Their ordered properties consist of organizationally demonstrable rational properties of indexical expressions and indexical actions. Those ordered properties are ongoing achievements of the concerted commonplace activities of the investigators. The demonstrable rationality of indexical expressions and indexical actions retains over the course of its managed production by members the character of ordinary, familiar, routinized, practical circumstances.

Does it *have* to be this way? Or is Official Style prose itself a form of professional grimacing and prancing? Using the PM as your guide, contrast the two passages. They make a revealing pair. Try to figure out what the second passage is trying to say and then revise it.

I've not found a satisfactory way to indicate prose rhythm in a printed book like *Revising Prose*. But try reading aloud these two passages we've examined, one after the other. Don't hurry. And don't read them in a monotone. Let the pitch and timbre of your voice vary. Try out various combinations of pitch, stress, and timing. (There are several ways to read the Phibbs passage, for example.) You can mark pitch variation with a wavy up-and-down line above the text, for a start. And mark musical rests (#, ##, ###) after each phrase and sentence. Read each passage aloud and have someone time you, observe where you pause and for how long. The first passage projects a recognizable voice; it is literally "readable." The second passage, academic prose at its most voiceless, is obviously meant to be read—skimmed—silently.

A Voice from the '60s

Prose varies widely in the performance instructions that it gives. Official Style academic prose gives very few. The voice has nowhere to go, no natural place to rise and fall, hurry and pause. Metronome prose: tick-tock, tick-tock, tick-tock. For extreme contrast, consider now a trip down prose nostalgia lane which offers lots of performance instructions. A sociology professor has taped a hippie guru telling us what it was like at Big Sur in the now-far-distant 1960s. Try marking the performance instructions; underline, double underline, use quotation marks, whatever.

When I first got up there, it was a real romantic kind of picture. Man, it was kind of foggy. There were those really beautiful people—men, women, kids, dogs and cats, and campfires. It seemed quiet and stable. And I really felt like love was about me. I thought, "This is the place, man. It was happening. I don't have to do it. I would just kind of fit in and do my thing and that would be like a groove."

After we were there about fifteen or twenty minutes, I heard the people bitching and moaning. I listened to it for awhile and circulated around to hear more about it, and, man, I couldn't believe it. Here they were secure in their land—beautiful land, where they could be free—and all these people were doing was bitching and moaning. I thought, "Oh, shit, man! Do I have to go into this kind of shit again where I gotta step in and get heavy and get ratty and get people to start talking? Do I have to get them to be open and get in some dialogue and get some communication going and organization? What the ———— is wrong with the leadership here, that this kind of state of affairs is happening? And why do I have to do it again? Man, I'm through with it. I just got through with hepatitis and double pneumonia and . . . ———— it!" Then I really felt bad.[2]

This is speech, for a start. Hippie speech, heavily syncopated speech, sliding quickly over interim syllables from heavy stress to heavy stress: "first," "romantic," "foggy," "really," "love." Once you know the syncopated pattern, it is easy to mark up a passage like this. But if you don't know the pattern? Imagine yourself a foreigner trying to read this passage with a natural emphasis. It does sometimes give natural rhythmic clues. "This is the *place*, man. It was *happening*. I don't *have* to do it." The arrangement of the words underscores the sense—the scene has become the actor and the actor the scene. So, too, the alliterative repetition of "go into," "gotta step in," "get heavy," "get ratty," "get people" gives us a clear performance clue. But the passage by itself does not include a full guide to its performance. (You needed to be part of the scene to talk this talk like a native. Hippie speech was an *argot*, a special way of speaking used to dramatize a special way of living. The guru quoted above hadn't always

[2]Lewis Yablonsky, *The Hippie Trip* (New York: Pegasus, 1968), p. 91.

talked this way. I know—he was in my class at Yale before the 1960s "came down.")

THE TRADITIONAL WAY TO PERFORM PROSE

How can prose include a performance guide, anyway? Especially complex prose of the sort the Official Style usually embodies? In the past, it has done so by a different route, by building up patterns of repetition, balance, antithesis, and parallelism. This package of systemic controls, usually called a "periodic sentence," has been the traditional way to control a long, complex sentence since classical Greece. The periodic style has been what we might call the "good" Official Style in Western stylistic history. It has striven for the Official attributes of public formality, authoritative impressiveness, solemnity even, but in a way that emphasizes voice rather than etiolating it. It represents true solemnity, a counter statement to the prose we have been revising. It designs a long sentence under strict control, not a shopping bag stuffed with words.

Any discussion of the Official Style should consider at least one instance of its legitimate ancestor, the periodic style. Here is an example by the eighteenth-century master of the periodic style in English, Samuel Johnson. He speaks about his design in compiling the first dictionary of the English language.

> When I am animated by this wish [to honor his country], I look with pleasure on my book, however defective, and deliver it to the world with the spirit of a man that has endeavoured well. That it will immediately become popular I have not promised to myself: a few wild blunders, and risible absurdities, from which no work of such multiplicity was ever free, may for a time furnish folly with laughter, and harden ignorance in contempt; but useful diligence will at last prevail, and there never can be wanting some who distinguish desert; who will consider that no dictionary of a living tongue ever can be perfect, since while it is hastening to publication, some words are budding, and some falling away; that a whole life cannot be spent upon syntax

and etymology, and that even a whole life would not be sufficient; that he, whose design includes whatever language can express, must often speak of what he does not understand; that a writer will sometimes be hurried by eagerness to the end, and sometimes faint with weariness under a task, which *Scaliger* compares to the labours of the anvil and the mine; that what is obvious is not always known, and what is known is not always present; that sudden fits of inadvertency will surprize vigilance, slight avocations will seduce attention, and casual eclipses of the mind will darken learning; and that the writer shall often in vain trace his memory at the moment of need, for that which yesterday he knew with intuitive readiness, and which will come uncalled into his thoughts to-morrow.[3]

We don't write prose like this anymore, and we are not used to reading it. The diagrammatic analysis in Figure 1 should help a modern reader *visualize* the structure. It works by adding elements in parallel:

> I   look with pleasure on my book, and
>   deliver it to the world

The parallel elements often create a contrast:

> some words are   budding
> and some   falling away

Or a repetitive list:

> *sudden fits of inadvertency*   will surprize vigilance,
> *slight avocations*   will seduce attention, and
> *casual eclipses of the mind*   will darken learning;

Often the antitheses form the antithetical pattern, called *chiasmus* (*chiasmus* comes from the Greek letter X, which is called "chi").

[3]From *Preface to the English Dictionary* in *Johnson: Prose and Poetry*, ed. Mona Wilson (Cambridge: Harvard University Press, 1967), pp. 322–323.

When I am animated by this wish [to honor his country],
  I look with pleasure on my book,
    however defective,
  and deliver it to the world
    with the spirit of a man that has endeavoured well.
That it will immediately become popular I have not promised to myself:
  a few wild blunders, and risible absurdities,
    from which no work of such multiplicity was ever free,
  may for a time   <u>furnish folly</u>   with <u>laughter,</u>
      and   <u>harden ignorance</u>   in <u>contempt</u>;
but useful diligence will at last prevail,
and **there never can be wanting some**
  <u>who</u> **distinguish desert;**
  <u>who</u> **will consider**
    that no dictionary of a living tongue ever can be perfect,
      since
          while it is hastening to publication,
            <u>some</u> words are   <u>budding,</u>
          and <u>some</u>   <u>falling away;</u>
    that <u>a whole life</u> cannot be <u>spent</u> upon syntax and etymology, and
    that <u>even a whole life</u> would not <u>be sufficient</u>;
    that he,
      whose design includes   <u>whatever</u> language can <u>express,</u>
        must often speak of   <u>what</u> he does not   <u>understand</u>;
    that a writer will <u>sometimes</u> be hurried by <u>eagerness to the end,</u>
        and <u>sometimes</u> faint   with <u>weariness under a task,</u>
            which *Scaliger* compares to the labours
            of the anvil and the mine;
    that   <u>what is obvious</u>   is <u>not always *known,*</u>
    and   <u>what is *known*</u>   is <u>not always present</u>;
    that
        <u>sudden fits of inadvertency</u>   <u>will surprize vigilance,</u>
        <u>slight avocations</u>   <u>will seduce attention,</u>
      and <u>casual eclipses of the mind</u>   <u>will darken learning</u>; and
    that the writer shall often in vain trace his memory
            at the moment of need,
       for that   <u>which yesterday</u> he knew with *intuitive readiness,* and
           <u>which</u> will come *uncalled* into his thoughts <u>to-morrow.</u>

Figure 1

What is <u>obvious</u>   is not always <u>known</u> and

What is <u>known</u>   is not always <u>obvious.</u>

The Official Style often embodies *lists*. The periodic style will hang its list of elements from a single lead word:

> **who** *will distinguish*
> **who** *will consider*

Or:

> **that** *no dictionary*
> **that** *a whole life*
> **that** *even a whole life*
> **that** *he*
> **that** *a writer*
> **that** *what is obvious*
> **that** *sudden fits*

These clear and repeated shapes *visualize* meaning, give the voice a set of *performing instructions*. In Figure 2, simply by using three sizes of type, I indicate the obvious stresses. Notice how the *voice* plays a counterpoint over the *shape*, sometimes reinforcing it and sometimes creating a different pattern. It is the absence of this counterpoint, more often than not, that makes the Official Style so insipidly lifeless.

Whether you relish periodic prose as I do or not, you ought to try in your own writing to give equally good performance instructions to the voice. And, in your long sentences, to maintain equally good syntactic and stylistic control. For, again, that is what sentence length, rhythm, and sound are—a series of instructions, of

When I am animated by this wish [to honor his country],

    I look with pleasure on my book,

        however defective,

    and deliver it to the world

        with the spirit of a man that has endeavoured well.

That it will immediately become popular I have not promised to myself:

    a few wild blunders, and risible absurdities,

        from which no work of such multiplicity was ever free,

    may for a time furnish folly   with laughter,

        and harden ignorance in contempt;

but useful diligence will at last prevail,

and there never can be wanting some

  who distinguish desert;

  who will consider

      that no dictionary of a living tongue ever can be perfect,

        since

          while it is hastening to publication,

          some words are budding,

        and some   falling away;

      that a whole life cannot be spent upon syntax and etymology, and

      that even a whole life would not be sufficient;

      that he,

        whose design includes   whatever language can   express,

        must often speak of what he does not   understand;

      that a writer will sometimes be hurried by eagerness to the end,

        and sometimes faint   with weariness under a task,

          which *Scaliger* compares to the labours

          of the anvil and the mine;

    that   what is obvious   is not always *known*,

    and   what is *known*   is not always present;

    that

      sudden fits of inadvertency   will surprize vigilance,

      slight avocations   will seduce attention,

    and casual eclipses of the mind   will darken learning; and

    that the writer shall often in vain trace his memory

        at the moment of need,

    for that   which yesterday he knew with *intuitive readiness*, and

        which will come *uncalled* into his thoughts tomorrow.

Figure 2

controls, for how your sentence should be performed. And if your readers take pleasure in performing your prose, you have them on your side. They are acting in your play.

We've seen how sentences become shapeless when the voice goes out of them. Prose that is not voiced becomes shapeless and unemphatic in the same way that an unexercised muscle loses its tone. And it works the other way, too. If we do not look at a piece of prose, attempt to perform it, we'll cease to hear real voices, our own and others', when we speak. Writing and speaking form a spiral. If they intensify each other, the spiral goes up. If they don't, each drives the other down.

Addendum: My "best try" revision of a passage that appears earlier in this chapter:

Original:
Rhythm in a sequence is that property of a sequence of events in time which produces in the mind of the observer the impression of proportion between the directions of the several events or groups of events of which the sequence is composed.

Revision:
Rhythm in a sequence shows the observer the proportions between the events that compose the sequence. (LF 63%)

4

Skotison!

The great Roman rhetorician Quintilian tells of a rhetoric teacher who taught his pupils to make everything they said intentionally obscure. *Skotison!*, he would tell them in Greek: *Darken it!* Successful obscurity elicited this praise from the teacher: "So much the better: even I could not understand it!" A later Latin writer, Ausonius, confessed to a similar relish for obscurity: "I might tell thee outright; but for more pleasure I will talk in mazes and with speech drawn out get full enjoyment." And, in the eighteenth century, Samuel Johnson wrote in an essay (*Idler*, 36) of the same delight in intentional obscurity: "There is a mode of style for which I know not that the masters of oratory have yet found a name, a style by which the most evident truths are so obscured that they can no longer be perceived, and the most familiar propositions so disguised that they cannot be known. Every other kind of eloquence is the dress of sense, but this is the mask. . . ." In my *Handlist of Rhetorical Terms* (University of California Press, second edition, 1991), I call this love of obscurity, this cultivation of darkness, *Skotison*— "Darken it!"

Eighteenth-century English poetry was especially fond of darkening and employed a special style, a "poetic diction," to create it. Alexander Pope parodied this false poetic sublimity in the satire *Peri Bathous: The Art of Sinking in Poetry* (1728), which supplies plain-language translations for poetic darkenings.

Poetic Diction	Plain English
For whom thus rudely pleads my loud-tongued gate, That he may enter?	Who knocks at the door?
The wooden guardian of our privacy Quick on its axle turn.	Shut the door.

Bring forth some remnant of the
    Promethean theft,
Quick to expand th'inclement air
    congealed
By *Boreas'* rude breath.
	Light the fire.

Apply thine engine to the
    spongy door,
Set *Bacchus* from his glassy prison
    free.
	Uncork the bottle.

Putting on the style in this way has always carried with it, then, the germ of parody. We have been hard at it translating the Official Style into plain English, dragging it out into the daylight by the scruff of the neck. For a change of pace, let's change direction. We'll see what it is like to put plain sense into bureaucratic language. Try parody as an analytic tool.

PARODY

Winston Churchill can show us how it is done. An American general once asked him to read the draft of a speech. "Too many passives and too many zeds," Churchill commented. Asked to explain his comment, Churchill said:

> Too many Latinate polysyllabics like "systematize, prioritize, finalize." And then the passives. What if I had said—instead of "We shall fight on the beaches"—"Hostilities will be engaged with our adversary on the coastal perimeter"?

"We shall fight on the beaches" rallied England to its Finest Hour. The Official Style's "Hostilities will be engaged with our adversary on the coastal perimeter," would have elicited first a "Huh?" and then probably a "Not by me they won't."

Some years ago, the American literary critic Lionel Trilling wrote: "A spectre haunts our culture. It is that people will eventually be unable to say 'We fell in love and married . . . but will, as a matter of course, say, 'Their libidinal impulses being reciprocal, they integrated their individual erotic drives and brought them within the same frame of reference.'" We've not got there yet, but we're close. So, now, the preacher begins his sermon with 'Had Moses not interfaced with Pharaoh. . . .' So now the lawyer resigns as chief of staff of Congress's Joint Tax Committee not because *it pays badly* but because 'while this job is clearly the best job in America for a tax lawyer, *one of the unfortunate downsides is that it causes one to be fiscally challenged.*' (I didn't make this up, truly.) So now the director of marketing for General Motors: 'We still don't know how good the new vehicles are because we have been so availability-constrained.' What he meant was, 'We don't know how well the new cars will sell because we haven't made enough yet to find out."

A humor website offers an Official Style version of the 23rd Psalm. Here's the *King James Version* first:

> The Lord is my shepherd; I shall not want.
> He maketh me to lie down in green pastures:
> He leadeth me beside the still waters.
> He restoreth my soul.
> He leadeth me in the paths of righteousness for his name's sake.
> Yea, though I walk through the valley of the shadow of death.
> I will fear no evil: for thou art with me;
> Thy rod and thy staff they comfort me.
> Thou preparest a table before me in the presence of mine enemies.
> Thou anointest my head with oil; my cup runneth over.
> Surely goodness and mercy shall follow me all the days of my life;
> And I will dwell in the house of the Lord for ever.

Look at all those active, transitive verbs: make, lead, restore, fear, comfort. And the actor is clear, a Lord who is first "He" and then, as we draw closer to Him, "thou." And we dwell in a world of physical reality—shepherd, green pastures, still waters, rod, staff, table—as we move from green pastures through a dreadful valley into the house of the Lord.

Here is how a bureaucrat makes the same journey:

> The Lord and I are in a shepherd-sheep situation, and I am in a position of negative need.
>
> He prostrates me in a green-belt grazing area, and conducts me directionally parallel to a nontorrential aqueous liquid.
>
> He restores to original satisfaction levels my psychological makeup.
>
> Notwithstanding the fact that I make ambulatory progress through the nonilluminated interhill mortality slot . . . terror sensations shall not be observed within me due to the proximity of the omnipotence.
>
> Your pastoral walking aid and quadruped pickup unit introduce me into a pleasurific mood state.
>
> You design and produce a nutrient-bearing furniture-type structure in the context of noncooperative elements, and my beverage utensil experiences a volume crisis.
>
> You enact a head-related folk ritual utilizing vegetable extracts.
>
> Surely it must be an ongoing nondeductible fact that your interrelational, emphatical, and nonvengeful capacities will pursue me as their target focus for the duration of this nondeath period.
>
> And I will possess tenant rights in the housing unit of the Lord on a permanently open-ended time basis.

We have here a *skotison* stylist of the first aqueous liquid. Type a phrase-by-phrase comparison of the parody with the original and try to describe exactly how the Official Style has been used. Or pick another psalm—Psalm 24 would be fun—and try your hand.

The Official Stylist never uses one simple word when a deluge of Latinate ones will do. Classical rhetoricians called this inflationary technique *amplification.* I downloaded from the Internet the following amplification of "Merry Christmas and Happy New Year."

Please accept with no obligation, implied or implicit, my best wishes for an environmentally conscious, socially responsible, low stress, non-addictive, gender neutral, celebration of the winter solstice holiday, practiced within the most enjoyable traditions of the religious persuasion of your choice, or secular practices of your choice, with respect for the religious/secular persuasions and/or traditions of others, or their choice not to practice religious or secular traditions at all, and a fiscally successful, personally fulfilling, and medically uncomplicated recognition of the onset of the generally accepted calendar year 1999, but not without due respect for the calendars of choice of other cultures whose contributions to society have helped make America great (not to imply that America is necessarily greater than any other country or is the only "AMERICA" in the western hemisphere), and without regard to the race, creed, color, age, physical ability, religious faith, choice of computer platform, or sexual preference of the wishee.

The parody reflects a fear that often drives the Official Stylist into hiding: Offend no one. How to be sure you don't? *Skotison!*

SELF-PARODIES

Sometimes Official Stylists parody themselves by translating their Official Style into plain English. Here's an example that says the same thing in two sentences, first in Official Style buzzwords and then in plain English.

Most analytically important, what are the metrics by which one assesses the course and pace of Iraq's central trend lines? How do we decide how we are doing?

The writer can write in both styles but wants to take no chances. He knows the official handshake even if he doesn't always use it.

Sometimes a bureaucracy supplies its own plain-language translation. The U.S. Office of Education once did so inadvertently (1971), when it issued Official Style definitions of plain words. Here are two examples. Want to say "activity" in the Official Style? Here's how you do it:

> Allocation of personnel and logistic resources to accomplish an iden-
> tifiable objective. Activities constitute the basis for defining personnel
> assignments and for scheduling system operations.

Want to say "need"? Here's how you do it in the U.S. Office of Education:

> A discrepancy or differential between "what is" and "what should
> be" (i.e. "what is required" or "what is desired"). In educational
> planning, "need" refers to problems rather than solutions, to the
> student "product" rather than to the resources for achieving that prod-
> uct, to the ends of education rather than to the means for attaining
> those ends.

Such translations are rare, though. Far more often we face the Official Style with no translation to help. The scholarly journal *Literature and Philosophy* sponsors a yearly "bad writing" contest in which readers send it samples of the worst prose they have encountered during the year. Three prize winners follow, all wonderful examples of *skotison*. Each is a single sentence.

A Marxist social critic:

> The triumphant moment in which a new systemic dominant gains
> ascendancy is therefore only the diachronic manifestation of a con-
> stant struggle for the perpetuation and reproduction of its dominance,
> a struggle which must continue throughout its life course, accompa-
> nied at all moments by the systemic or structural antagonism of those
> older and newer modes of production that resist assimilation or seek
> deliverance from it.

A philosopher:

> Indeed dialectical critical realism may be seen under the aspect of
> Foucauldian strategic reversal of the unholy trinity of Parmenidean/
> Platonic/Aristotelean provenance; of the Cartesian-Lockean-Humean-Kantian

paradigm, of foundationalisms (in practice, fideistic foundationalisms) and irrationalisms (in practice, capricious exercises of the will-to-power or some other ideologically and/or psycho-somatically buried source) new and old alike; of the primordial failing of western philosophy, ontological monovalence, and its close ally, the epistemic fallacy with its ontic dual; of the analytic problematic laid down by Plato, which Hegel served only to replicate in his actualist monovalent analytic reinstatement in transfigurative reconciling dialectical connection, while in his hubristic claims for absolute idealism he inaugurated the Comtean, Kierkegaardian and Nietzschean eclipses of reason, replicating the fundaments of positivism through its transmutation route to the superidealism of a Baudrillard.

A literary critic:

When interpreted from within the ideal space of the myth-symbol school, Americanist masterworks legitimized hegemonic understanding of American history expressively totalized in the metanarrative that had been reconstructed out of (or more accurately read into) these masterworks.

Unintentional self-parody of this sort is not uncommon in the modern academic world. Since *Revising Prose* first appeared in 1979, academic disciplines have grown more Official, not less, and prided themselves on their increasing obscurity. The social sciences, which formerly led the way, have ceded pride of place to the humanities, where the special field called "literary theory" has devised a special language of its own, of which these passages seem to be examples. Students are assigned and forced to imitate acres of such stuff.

I won't revise these passages, since, overall, I cannot understand them. In fact, other readers, more qualified than I in the disciplines invoked, have been equally mystified. If you've ever taken a course in one of these areas, though, you might try your hand at it.

Surely, mystification—*skotison*—is the main aim here. Defenders of mystifying styles sometimes offer just this argument. Writers who make readers puzzle out a meaning give their readers better value for money. Digging up the meaning is half the fun. Obscurity ensures rarity. To object that you can't understand such prose misses the point. It belongs to another genre altogether, *the rhetoric of display*. It aims to display the writers' knowledge, their in-group status. They *know the secret handshake* and all the arcane terms, and can display them in a simulacrum of English syntax.

When Official Styles develop in a closed professional field, they turn in on themselves and become more interested in display and less in argument. Anyone who writes with an eye toward ordinary understanding is stigmatized as a "popularizer." It has happened before and—given the persistence of ego, fear, fashion, and our human love of euphemism—will happen again. When you grow up in such a style, and nowadays every American student does, plain prose makes you feel undressed. As a student, and as a mature professional too, you want to imitate the accepted writers in your field, and they write in various professional dialects of the Official Style. Naturally, piously, you want to imitate them. You assume that the rhetoric of display substitutes for argument. And often, if you get it right, you are right. Stylistic imitation proves that you've joined the club, and you get a good grade. Or a published article.

How to behave in an Official Style world, whether to persist in trying to make ordinary sense or give in to the *skotison*, I will discuss in the "Why Bother?" chapter. But we all should be aware that the Official Style, in the highest stages of its development, not only discourages plain sense but also abandons it altogether for the pleasures of display. Understanding this development spares readers who want to make out the plain sense—the readers of this book—much vexation of spirit.

A PAUSE FOR REVIEW

Let's pause to review the Official Style that stands behind *skotison*.

It hides *actor* and *action* in passive and impersonal constructions. Never "I decided" but always "It was decided that. . . ."

It displaces the action from simple verb into a complex construction: "I see" becomes "A visionary ability can be obtained which permits. . . ."

It uses a Latinate diction—all those "zed" verbs like "prioritize" and all those "shun" nouns like "prioritization."

It adores the slow sentence start, the long windup while the writer thinks up something to say: "One can easily see that in confronting a situation of this sort. . . ."

It follows faithfully a formula of prepositional phrases + "is" + more prepositional phrases. "The fact of the matter in a case of this sort is that. . . ."

These strings of prepositional phrases make it *shapeless.* The eye can offer no help to the sense.

Because it offers the voice no chance to emphasize or harmonize, you cannot read it out loud. It is, literally, unspeakable.

It takes twice as long (at least) as its plain English translation. In the fullness of its best, it embodies the attitudes, and complacent habits of inaction, of a large, impersonal, arbitrary bureaucracy.

Finally, the Official Style is *euphemistic.* Everyone sees this now, and laughs at it. Buzzword indexes abound. Rats become "small faunal species," smells dress up as "olfactory impacts." Or, in the new "politically correct" versions: "Short"="vertically challenged." "Fat"="possessing an alternative body image." "Dumb"="negatively gifted." (Confession: I made that one up.) Correct grammar becomes "ethnocentric white patriarchal restructuring of language." (I did not make that one up.) Every misbehaving child has "oppositional defiance disorder." The Official Style, in whatever new dress, always dresses up in a special terminology.

But if the Official Style has become a standing joke, why does it continue to thrive?

WHY DOES THE OFFICIAL STYLE THRIVE?

And thrive it does. It grows ever stronger. Government, in spite of many "privatizings," just keeps growing. Professional specialization grips our lives with an ever stronger hand, and professional languages grow ever more arcane and incomprehensible. Business organizations merge into ever larger, and therefore more bureau-cratic, conglomerations. Even the language of business—where, you would think, a plain style would be most prized—has grown Official. As a book on management gurus put it: "There seems to be something in the water in business schools or at management conferences that destroys people's capacity to speak plainly or write clearly."[1] The "something in the water" is *skotison!* Just when attention has become the most precious commodity in our econ-omy, we are like to drown in logorrhea and boredom. The waste of time, space, and human attention, the hours and days of mysti-fied, head-scratching puzzlement, seem beyond reckoning. And they are not necessary. Anybody can learn to revise the Official Style into a plain dynamic one. It does indeed take some effort, as the previous chapters teach. But it saves even more. Why, then, do we put up with the Official Style?

Ego leads the pack. The Official Style is, or is commonly thought to be, more imposing. It speaks with organizational authority. Like a football helmet and shoulder pads, it makes the writer look taller, wider, more intimidating.

Fear contends with ego for the starring role. If you work in a large organization, standing out from the crowd can kill you. Don't get identified with *any* action, because if it goes wrong, you'll get the blame. Imitate the style you encounter all around you. "Diversity" has no place in the world of prose style.

Litigation comes not far behind. In so pervasively litigious a society as ours, incomprehensible prose has come into its own as a protection against being sued. People are less likely to sue you if they can't understand what you have said. And you can put up a better defense if you can argue that you haven't said it any-way. The Official Style serves both purposes equally well.

Oddly enough, print itself must take some of the blame. It per-mits no direct voice. Its presentational conventions—black-and-white, continuous lineation, constant typeface—allow only indirect emphasis. Acres of Official Style print have spawned a new kind of reading—speed reading—which encourages reading only for a

---

[1]John Micklethwait and Adrian Wooldridge, *The Witch Doctors* (Times Books, 1996), p. 12.

key island of significance in a sea of ritualistic verbosity. Ever since Marshall McLuhan called print a "visual" medium, we've thought of it that way, but at its most profound level it doesn't work on the visual cortex at all. Print aims to be invisible, unnoticed by the eye, so that we can concentrate on the *thought*. A mode of presentation like electronic text, which invokes both eye and ear, makes the Official Style hard to bear.

Professional mystification plays a strong role. We might call this the collective ego of our ever-increasing interpretive bureaucracy. The Official Style comes in a variety of dialects, but they are all professional languages. The language of the law came first, as old as written history, with the Greek and Latin patois of medical terminology a close second. Governmental bureaucracies have always cherished a special language to make them more priestly and witch-doctorish, and hence more authoritative. They spoke the language of a deep mystery. When the current academic and professional specializations came to the fore a century ago, they each created a dialect of the Official Style to prove that they were scientific. The less scientific they were, the more Official their style.

Self-mystification plays more than a bit part. If a bureaucracy uses the Official Style for very long, it begins to fool *itself.* After this happens—and it has happened in every government bureau and academic discipline—plain English looks like *satire.* If you do a *Revising Prose* number on an Official Style report, you are pointing out that the emperor has no clothes on. You are writing satire, and satire is a dangerous business. *Revising Prose* reader, be warned!

We ought not, though, close this brief discussion of *skotison* on a churlish, puritanical note. After all, *skotison* springs from linguistic play as well as humorless self-importance. We all enjoy the special language we use for our special concerns. The computer industry, which has not usually been accused of taking itself too seriously, started out with a special language it had to invent for a new world. It then started using it for ordinary life, so that every meeting became an "interface" and every dullard a "slow chip." It uses the euphemistic jargon of political correctness, as often as not, with humor and irony. The Official Business

Style that is taught in schools of management spawns a playful jargon. From an article in the *Los Angeles Times*, I learned that the CEO of a much-touted startup, when he had to report a huge fourth-quarter loss, changed his title to "Visionary." The former chairman of a coffee company styled himself "Chief Coffee Officer." "Evangelist" and "Vibe Guy" have joined COO, CEO, CFO, and all those square titles on rectangular business cards. And you make a plan by "dimensionalizing," look ahead by "helicoptering," and read between the lines by seeking out "white space opportunities." Sometimes, especially if your ox isn't being gored, it is more fun to sit back, put your feet up, and savor the throughput. *Skotison!*

5

Business Prose

OK. From parodies back to business. What should business writing be like? It ought to be fast, concrete, and responsible. It should show *someone acting*, doing something to or for someone else. Business life offers few occasions for the descriptive set-piece; it chronicles history in the making, depicts someone working on matter or with people. It seldom relates abstract concepts for the fun of it; abstractions occur as parts of a problem to be solved. Business prose ought, therefore, to be *verb-dominated* prose, lining up actor, action, and object in a causal chain, and lining them up fast.

In recent times, though, business prose has been engulfed by the Official Style. It comes at business from government regulation, legal threats, economic forecasts, and MBA-trained consultant advice. No wonder business has started to sound bureaucratic. We are all bureaucrats these days, or shortly will be, whether we work for the government directly or soldier on in the private sector and get our government money through grants, contracts, or subsidies. And even if—especially if—we belong to that shrinking part of the private sector that remains truly private, we'll be for certain filling out government forms, having OSHA for lunch whether we invited her or not.

Business writing seems to be going in one direction and management practice in another. As management becomes more horizontal, less layered, the language MBAs and business gurus use to describe it becomes more bureaucratic and hierarchical. There does indeed seem to be something in the water in business.

SOMETHING IN THE WATER

That something is the Official Style in all its varieties. For example:

> An extension of the concept of wireless access to commercial information services is the provision of the same type of access to corporate databases.

Our regular breakout:

An extension
of the concept
of wireless access
to commercial information services
is the provision
of the same type
of access
to corporate databases.

The root *action* seems to lie buried in "extension." Let's start from there.

> Something *extends* something.

OK. What can be extended? "Wireless access."

> Wireless access can be extended from commercial databases to corporate ones.

It still doesn't make sense. The writer seems to have meant "Wireless access to commercial databases suggests access to corporate ones as well." If so, both *actor* and *action* are so deeply buried it requires a root canal to find them. This sentence shows thought not only imprisoned by the Official Style but stultified by it.

And here's another, simple-seeming enough, from a university executive.

> In light of the pervasive problem of overcrowding at UC Lone Pine, providing another coffeehouse on campus would offer the university's growing population some kind of compensatory convenience.

Consider, first, all the *possible* actions this sentence invokes:

pervades
overcrowds
provides
offers
grows
compensates

The reader can't decide which should predominate. And who is *acting* in this mixture of possible actions? The "pervasive problem"? "UC Lone Pine"? "another coffeehouse"? To decipher a sentence like this, we have to take it part by part. Let's start with the opener:

In light
of the pervasive problem
of overcrowding
at UC Lone Pine

Notice how this string of prepositional phrases delays the real action of the sentence? The Paramedic Method views prepositional phrases as an entrance into a sentence, a place to begin. Can we get rid of them here? Let's try a preemptive strike: "Overcrowded Lone Pine." Three words instead of ten. And a natural *subject*—UC Lone Pine. OK. Now what *action*, what *verb*, fits UC Lone Pine? Now it is easy to see: Lone Pine *needs* something. Now that actor and action are clear, the object is clear, too—*another coffeehouse*.

Original:
In light of the pervasive problem of overcrowding at UC Lone Pine, providing another coffeehouse on campus would offer the university's growing population some kind of compensatory convenience. (28 words)

Intermediate stage:

~~In light of the pervasive problem of~~ overcrowding ~~at~~ UC Lone Pine, ~~providing~~ another coffeehouse ~~on campus would offer the university's growing population some kind of compensatory convenience.~~

Revision:

Overcrowded UC Lone Pine needs another coffeehouse. (7 words)

Seven words instead of twenty-eight. A lard factor of 75%. Now put this morbid obesity back into the world of action. Imagine an executive who *thinks like this*, can't make a simple diagnosis, take a simple action. I'm not talking here about the standard genres of business writing, the letter, job-application, etc. I'm talking about the means of conscious thought and action at their fundamental level. As I've said before in this book and will say again, this is not a small mistake. Imagine a business day in which every action takes 75% longer than it needs to.

Management must make decisions, take action. The worst thing you can do is offer a blurred menu of possible actions. It is easy to do, fatally easy:

Hypertext was invented to facilitate the process *of* navigating *through* a presentation *of* a collection *of* interrelated topics.

Diagrammatically:

Hypertext was invented
to facilitate the process
of navigating
through a presentation
of a collection
of interrelated topics.

Again, notice the plethora of possible actions:

invent
facilitate
navigate

present
collect
interrelate

Surely *navigate* supplies the main action. The Official Style loves amplifying fillers like "facilitate" and "process." You can almost always get rid of them:

Hypertext was invented to ~~facilitate the process of~~ navigate . . .

Now for

through a presentation
of a collection
of interrelated topics.

This string of prepositional phrases says the same thing three times: a presentation of a collection of interrelated topics. If you insist on breaking up that prepositional phrase string, you soon see that all you need is "interrelated topics."

Original:
Hypertext was invented to facilitate the process of navigating through a presentation of a collection of interrelated topics. (18 words)

Revision:
Hypertext was invented to navigate through interrelated topics. (8 words; LF 55%)

Notice how boring and monotonous that string of prepositional phrases becomes? The sentence wants to describe a causal process, as so much of business writing does. What *caused* A? How to get from A to B to C? The Official Style always does its best to obscure a causal pattern or a chain of command. In this example, the chain runs from "hypertext" to "navigate" to "interrelated topics." *Navigate* is the crucial action. Action verbs should stand at the center of business discourse. You should always know who is acting, how, when, and toward whom or what.

In the next example, the writer can't bear to make clear any of these relationships.

> Dear Brad: We have had an acceptance of our offer of employment from the outstanding candidate for the position of regional marketing manager.

The string of prepositional phrases tips you off that something has gone badly wrong:

> We have had an acceptance
> *of* our offer
> *of* employment
> *from* the outstanding candidate
> *for* the position
> *of* regional marketing manager.

Where's the *action* here? The actor is clear—"We"—but what is the central action? What have "We" done? They have **hired** a new regional marketing manager and it isn't Brad. But "We" can't bring himself or herself to say so—"We have hired someone else as regional marketing manager" (9 words instead of 21; LF 54%). So this central action is blurred through the strings of prepositional phrases. But you don't soften bad news by stringing it out like saltwater taffy. In the next sentence, the writer continues to writhe within the confines of the Official Style's prepositional phrase strings.

> Nevertheless, I extend
> **to** you my very best wishes
> **for** a successful conclusion
> **to** your personal search
> **for** the right career path
> **for** you.

A "personal" search? What other kind is there? The right career path "for you." For who else? When I "extend my very best wishes," I "wish." The writer desperately wants to avoid saying the plain truth: "Nevertheless, I wish you success in your job search" (LF 62%). The Official Style provides the perfect vehicle for avoiding the plain truth—a truth that would be much kinder than Official Style flummery. It is those prepositional phrases that—in a sentence of the sort of which this is a type of—expose the real problem. Mark them up; they'll usually tell you where to begin.

Now, let's take this search for actor and action, for a detectable and responsible *chain of command* in a sentence, one step further.

> After reviewing the research and in light of the relevant information found within the context of the conclusions, we feel that there is definite need for some additional research to more specifically pinpoint our advertising and marketing strategies.

The standard formula: "is" + prepositional phrases fore and aft. And often a "to" infinitive sign joins the conga line.

> *After* reviewing the research and
> *in* light
> *of* the relevant information found
> *within* the context
> *of* the conclusions,

>   we feel that there **is** definite need

> *for* some additional research
> *to* more specifically pinpoint

>   our advertising and marketing strategies.

Where's the action? Who's kicking who? Well, the kicker is obviously "we." And the action? *Needing*—but buried in *there is definite need.* So the core of the sentence emerges as "We need more research." Let's try brutal subtraction before and after this central statement.

> ~~After reviewing the~~ research ~~and in light of the relevant information found within the context of~~ the conclusions, ~~we feel that there is~~

~~definite~~ need ~~for some additional~~ research to ~~more specifically~~ pinpoint our advertising and marketing strategies.

The revision then reads:

> The conclusions of previous research suggest that we need more research to pinpoint our advertising and marketing strategies.

Eighteen words instead of 38—LF 53%. Not bad—but wait a minute. How about "the conclusions of"? Do we need it? Why not:

> Previous research suggests that we need more research to pinpoint our advertising and marketing strategies. (LF 60%)

And this revision, as so often happens, suggests a further and more daring one:

> **has failed**
>
> Previous research ~~suggests that we need more research~~ to pinpoint our advertising and marketing strategies.

> Previous research has failed to pinpoint our advertising and marketing strategies. (LF 71%)

By now, of course, we've changed kicker and kickee and, to an extent, the meaning. But isn't the new meaning what the writer wanted to say in the first place? A previous failure has generated a subsequent need? And the new version *sounds* better, too. The awkward repetition of "research" has been avoided, and we've finally found the real first kicker, "previous research," and found out *what it was doing*—it "failed." We can now bring in the second kicker in an emphatic second sentence:

> Previous research has failed to pinpoint our advertising and marketing strategies. *We need to know more.*

No "is," no prepositional phrases, a LF of 58%, and the two actors and actions clearly sorted out.

This example illustrates an important truth. Revision proceeds by stages. You can't do it all at once and you learn nothing if you just say "too wordy" and throw it in the wastebasket. Again, the drill: Circle every form of "to be" (e.g., is, was, will be, seems to be) and every prepositional phrase. Then find the action and start rebuilding the sentence with that action. Two prepositional phrases in a row turn on the warning light, three make a problem, and four invite disaster. (As you read on, see if you catch me disregarding my own advice and revise accordingly.) With a little practice, sentences like:

> The role of markets is easily observed and understood when dealing with a simple commodity such as potatoes.

will turn into:

> A simple commodity like potatoes shows clearly how markets work.
> (LF 44%)

In a revision like this, aren't we doing just what the Toyota people taught the rest of the auto business about efficient assembly? Go through the whole line, find out what is really needed, what can be cut, shortened, rearranged. Find the *muda* and get rid of it.

ACTION PROGRAMS

Every sentence, after all, describes an action program. We can think of a sentence as an assembly line but we can also think of it as a *circuit diagram*, a mental circuit diagram. To stay in business, you must not lose sight of the energy flow, who is doing what to whom. The following sentence builds a series of resistors into the circuit by blurring every important action:

> The trend in the industry is toward self-manufacture by some companies of their own cans, and packing technology is changing packaging requirements so as not to require the typical heavy metal can.

First, notice that the sentence falls into two unrelated parts:

> The trend in the industry is toward self-manufacture by some companies of their own cans,
>> and
>
> packing technology is changing packaging requirements so as not to require the typical heavy metal can.

The two parts must bear some relation to each other; if not, why do they share the same sentence? What might it be? In cases like this, best to find the action in each half and then guess at the relationship between them.

So, the first half. Where's the *action*? Hidden down there in *self-manufacture*. Somebody is *making* something. Who is doing it? Who is the subject? We have a choice of three: *trend, industry, companies*. Easy to see the natural subject here: *companies*. We now have a clear circuit:

> Some companies make their own cans.

We know where the action is, who is kicking who. The dead-rocket opening, *The trend in the industry is toward = now*, and so we have:

> Some companies now make their own cans. (LF 53%)

The LF of 53% only begins to tell the story. The writer could not express a basic simple action, could not see who was acting or what the action was. And the stumbling approximation took twice as long.

Am I overemphasizing a trivial mistake? Suppose your company could save 50% of everything you spent on the written word, from paper, ink, and fax machines to employee reading time. And what of the mental processes of someone who cannot see, or explain, a simple business process? The idea of a *company* should pose no special intellectual challenge to a business person. Nor should *making*. Cans are not a space-age product. We're not talking about quantum theory or side-scanning radar. The gigantic wastage revealed by such a sentence (or half a sentence—we are not finished with it) comes in the *thinking* revealed. Thinking time costs a lot of money.

Now for the second half of the sentence:

> packing technology is changing packaging requirements so as not to require the typical heavy metal can.

Again, who's kicking who? Where is the *action*? We now know how to look at the surface of a sentence for anomalies, for resistors in the circuit. This writer tips us off by his redundancy: *requirements* and *require*. But at least we have a verb—*require*. Who or what is doing the requiring? Not, as the writer writes it, the *requirements*, since that means that the *requirements* are *requiring*, which is tautological and witless. No, our actor is *technology*. Now, at last, we have actor and action: *packing technology requires*. So we come to this:

> packing technology no longer requires a heavy metal can. (LF 44%)

At this point, we can contemplate the relationship between the two halves of the sentence. The writer did not specify a relationship, transferring that cost to the reader. My guess:

> Since packing technology no longer requires a heavy metal can, some companies now make their own.

Our lard factor, as chance would have it, scores a bull's-eye: 50%, 16 words instead of 32. But, again, the LF only uncurtains the problem. Prose models thought, and thought must account for events and the causal relationships between them, the causes and results that keep a business solvent. The Official Style attacks business at its heart—a knowledge of *what's happening.*

CONSULTANT MUDA

Now for an example from current business high fashion—the consultant's report. This consulting company was developing a "strategic market plan" for a bank.

> The purpose of an environmental scan is to obtain a general understanding of the external business environment we are currently in and expect to be in over the near-term. This may include any number of factors, but they are factors that may significantly impact the bank's business, either positively or negatively depending upon how we manage our way through them.

OK. Not hard to understand, but blurred, boring, and, my goodness, way too long. *Muda! Waste!* Let's do a PM diagram to diagnose the problem.

> The purpose
> *of* an environmental scan
> **is**
> *to* obtain a general understanding
> *of* the external business environment
> we are currently *in*
> and expect to be *in*
> *over* the near-term.
> **This** may include any number
> *of* factors,
> but they are **factors** that may significantly impact the bank's
> business, either positively or negatively
> depending upon how we manage our way through them.

I've taken two liberties to emphasize the Official Style formula: (1) I've included the infinitive sign "to" as if it were a preposition, since, here and usually, it acts like one in the Official Style; (2) I've put a drop shadow on "This" since we don't know what it refers to, and this blurred reference blurs the relationship between the two sentences. I've also drop-shadowed "factors" (no consultant's report is complete without "factors" and "strategic") because, if we don't know what "this" refers to, we don't know what the "factors" are.

Set to work with the PM. Identifying the prepositions and the "is" establishes the Official Style formula:

> Slow windup, with a prepositional phrase or two, ending with **is:**
> The purpose of an environmental scan **is** . . .
>
> A string of prepositions/infinitives following:
> to obtain . . . currently *in* . . . expect to be *in* . . . *over* . . . the near-term.

Actor and *action* have gone into hiding, as usual. The grammatical subject of the sentence is "purpose," but is "purpose" the central actor? No, it is *scan*. The passage wants to tell us what an "environmental scan" *does*. Where is the *action*? Hiding, too, in "to obtain a general understanding of." "To obtain a general understanding of" = "to understand." Now we have a central action—*understand*. We have changed a resistor that resists energy into a capacitor that stores it. But wait a minute. Who is obtaining the understanding? As written, it is the *scan*, but that makes no sense. The scan doesn't do the understanding, we do, using the scan. The writer has confused cause—*scan*—and effect—*understanding*. Applying the PM's first three rules diligently has allowed us to see what the problems are, where the sentence goes wrong.

OK. We do have an *actor*—an environmental scan. What is it *doing*? Well, it can't "obtain a general understanding," since only people can understand, not reports. What word might we use for "obtaining a general understanding of"? My favorite thesaurus[1] suggests: "observe, scrutinize, regard, contemplate, consider, review, study, examine, investigate, pore over, peruse, appraise, assess, size, up, survey," and many more. The language of plain discourse is rich beyond calculation. I'll go for "survey."

---

[1] J.I. Rodale, *The Synonym Finder* (Warner Books, 1978).

OK. We have—and it hasn't been easy—an *actor* and an *action*:

> An environmental scan surveys . . .

What does it survey? As written:

> the external business environment we are currently in and expect to be in over the near-term.

As always, take it a part at a time:

> the external business environment we are currently in = the current business environment
>
> and expect to be in over the near-term = foreseeable

Adding the two together gives us "the current and foreseeable business environment."

So we have this before-and-after photo:

Original:
The purpose of an environmental scan is to obtain a general under-standing of the external business environment we are currently in and expect to be in over the near-term. (29 words)

Revision:
An environmental scan surveys the current and foreseeable business environment. (10 words; LF 65%)

The lard factor exceeds our normative one half—65%. But more important, the revision has identified the real actor and the real action, and clarified the relationship between them.

Before we take on the second sentence from this consultant's report, let's reflect upon the first. Mistaking actor and action and the relationship between the two does not constitute a trivial error, a "matter of style." Business may not be war without the guns, as some say it is, but it does involve players and struggles between them. You should know who is doing what to whom.

To confuse the players and the game, cause and effect, constitutes a *big* mistake. And who is making it? A *business consultant.*
Somebody who is *advising someone else how to act,* advising
them, as a good economist should, how to allocate a scarce
resource more efficiently. And this advisor doesn't know who is
doing what to whom.

Now for the consultant's second sentence.

> This may include any number of factors, but they are factors that may
> significantly impact the bank's business, either positively or negatively
> depending upon how we manage our way through them.

The *actor?* "Factors," obviously. But "factor" is a *very* general
word (and a favorite in the Official Style—that's why I chose it for
"lard factor"). What *exactly* does it mean here? To find out that,
we must know what "This" is. "This," whatever it is, includes all
those "factors," and they are vital to the sentence. So "This" is
vital. But alas, it is a *This* this. It refers back to something in the
previous sentence but we don't know what. According to the
rules, it refers back to the noun most immediately preceding,
which would be "near-term." But that doesn't make much sense.
So what does it refer to? I'll indicate the "possible perps" as the
police like to say ("perp" = perpetrator).

> The purpose of an environmental scan is to obtain a general under-
> standing of the external business environment we are currently in
> and expect to be in over the near-term.

Does *This* refer to a general understanding or to the external business environment? Your guess is as good as mine. The reference
oscillates between the one and the other. I choose the "business
environment." Elements of the business environment affect
("impact" is the Official Style word for "affect" or "influence") the
bank's business. Somehow. So the sentence should read:

> [The business environment] may include any number of factors, but
> they are factors that may significantly impact the bank's business,
> either positively or negatively depending upon how we manage our
> way through them.

Wait a minute. Things get worse. There may be any number of factors (whatever they are) and they *may* affect, or may not, the bank's business, either up or down. Depending on what the bank does. At this point in the analysis, your mind begins to lose its bearings. The sentence, which aims to guide us, has lost us instead. The assembly line starts to run backwards. There are a bunch of factors, or may be, in the business environment and they may affect the bank, or may not, depending on what the bank does. So what else is new? Under the infarcted language lurks a trite commonplace:

> How these factors [or "this environment"] affect the bank's business depends on how the bank responds to them.

Now let's put the two sentences together:

> An environmental scan surveys the current and foreseeable business environment. How this environment affects the bank's business depends on how the bank responds to it. (25 words)

The original again:

> The purpose of an environmental scan is to obtain a general understanding of the external business environment we are currently in and expect to be in over the near-term. This may include any number of factors, but they are factors that may significantly impact the bank's business, either positively or negatively depending upon how we manage our way through them. (60 words)

A lard factor of 58%. But that factor only points toward the real trouble. The two sentences don't say much. The Official Style fools everybody connected with it—writer as well as reader—into thinking more has been thought and said (and paid for) than in fact has been. We're not talking about fancy phrases to make us feel important—"Return the handset to the cradle" instead of "hang up" or "achieve the desired velocity" instead of "go as fast as you want," or "the captain has elected to illuminate the seat-belt sign" (I've heard it, honestly) instead of "the captain has turned on the seat-belt sign." We are talking about deep self-delusion.

WRITING ABOUT BUSINESS WRITING

Now for another kind of consultant's report, from someone who teaches business writing. Teachers working in this field, like other academics, must publish articles, and these articles must be acceptable to two groups devoted to the Official Style: the MBA types and the empirical linguists. Not only how business is done but also how it is studied now goes forward in the Official Style. The following "about-business writing" example hides actor and action under a pond scum of passives, prepositions, verbs made into nouns, and Latinate "shun" words—institu*tion*alized, organ-iza*tions*, configura*tions*.

> With respect to institutionalized properties of organizations, our frame-work suggests that over time, the actions exercised by humans in the domains of media use, message structure, and language become habitual, and particular configurations of media, message structure, and language emerge and are invoked in certain circumstances to achieve some communicative intent.

Action? Action? Actor? Actor? What are they talking about? Let's deploy the PM to facilitate the analytical planning process:

1. Circle the prepositions.
2. Circle the "is" forms.
3. Find the *action*.
4. Put this action in a simple (not compound) active verb.
5. Start fast—no slow windups

OK, we invoke Rules 1 and 2:

> *With* respect *to* institutionalized properties *of* organizations, our framework suggests that *over* time, the actions exercised *by* humans

in the domains *of* media use, message structure, and language **become** habitual, and particular configurations *of* media, message structure, and language emerge and **are** invoked *in* certain circumstances *to* achieve some communicative intent. (51 words)

Now, Rule 3. Who is kicking who? Where's the *action*? It's almost impossible to see, but the sentence does contain two centers of power and we can start there:

actions become habitual
configurations of media . . . emerge and are invoked

In these two centers of power lurk six possible actions:

act
habituate
configure
emerge
invoke
achieve

Now—remember, we're working step by step—let's translate the individual phrases from the Official Style into English:

institutional properties of organizations = company habits

actions exercised by humans in the domains of media use, message structure, and language become habitual = people tend to express themselves in habitual ways

particular configurations of media, message structure, and language emerge and are invoked in certain circumstances to achieve some communicative intent = people tend to express themselves in habitual ways

Have I done the passage an injustice? I don't see how. The plain English for the whole passage, so far as I can see, must run something like this:

In large organizations, people tend to express themselves in habitual ways. (11 words; LF 78%)

You might then specify what those ways, those media, are. But you would have to name names, specific actors performing specific actions, people writing, speaking, sending e-mail, following accepted report forms, etc.

Anybody who has studied the social sciences has read acres of such prose. It may be all right for that kind of thinking—though I do not think so—but for business? As a model for business prose, I find a passage like this a little scary. It muddles the world of affairs, a place where *actions* and their *actors* must be clear and the causal relationships between them precise. It aims to fool writer and reader into thinking a cliché is a profundity. As we have seen so often before, the worst danger is the illusion that communication has occurred when it hasn't.

If business writing presents puzzles on the one hand and pretentious flapdoodle on the other, we'll never get any business done. What happens to the ordinary business of life in this world of loony language? If we don't know who the players are or what game they are playing, we really are in the marmalade. Deciphering such prose is possible, though, and using the PM, you'll soon be doing it quickly. Isn't getting on with your business twice as fast worth the effort? In working, as in the rest of life, it's a big help to know where the action is, who's kicking who. Nobody in his or her right mind *wants* to write prose like that we have exemplified here. Why keep tolerating it? Confusing your many hearers and readers costs a lot. Confusing yourself may cost much more.

Professional Prose

As professions mature and coalesce they develop their own special languages. They start out talking to a general audience but soon begin to close in upon themselves, talking only to each other. The more they do so, the closer their professional languages resemble one another, morph into the Official Style. But professional languages today can no longer talk only to themselves. Plain language laws insist that the law be discussed in prose ordinary people can understand. The medical profession feels the same pressures. Medical treatment costs so much we want to know exactly what is wrong with us, and the Internet has given us the means to find out for ourselves. Ritual mystification is no longer acceptable in law or medicine. Nor, and especially, in government. Nor, and again especially, in economics. Nor in all the other scholarly conversations that so immediately affect our day-to-day life. All are feeling pressures to explain themselves in ways open to common understanding.

Professions have now become professional bureaucracies, but accountability demands that these bureaucracies must become interpretive bureaucracies. They must move outside their special language and talk to ordinary people. It is as important, now, to explain to people the significance of what you do as it is to do it. No profession is exempt from this accountability; the trial lawyers, if nobody else, will see to that.

Revising Prose shows how to do this kind of translating. Such translation, let me repeat, also provides the best way to keep the interior bureaucratic conversation from degenerating into a mutual exchange of buzzwords in which everybody says "You know?" and nobody really knows. Explaining what you do to outsiders requires that you understand it yourself.

A strong counterforce still fights against this interpretive accountability. At the end of the nineteenth century, the learned professions coalesced into special bodies and, as they did so, began to turn inward and talk to one another using a special language for an increasingly specialized inquiry. The acerbic Nobel economist George Stigler caught this change perfectly, in "The Intellectual and the Marketplace":

> Less than a century ago a treatise on economics began with a sentence such as, "Economics is a study of mankind in the ordinary business of life." Today it will often begin, "This unavoidably lengthy treatise is devoted to an examination of an economy in which the second derivatives of the utility function possess a finite number of discontinuities. To keep the problem manageable, I assume that each individual consumes only two goods, and dies after one Robertsonian week. Only elemental mathematical tools such as topology will be employed incessantly."

There are some private jokes going on here, but you get the picture. After a lifetime of such prose, you can forget how to address a general public even if you want to.

A NOBEL ECONOMIST

Here is another Nobel economist, writing an op-ed piece for the *Wall Street Journal.*

> The perpetuation of open-access societies like the United States in a world of continuous novel change raises a fundamental institutional dilemma at the heart of the issue of economic development and of successful dynamic change. By uncertainty, we mean that we do not know what is going to happen in the future, and that condition

characterizes the world we have been creating. How can our minds make sense of new and novel conditions? The answer that in fact has proven successful in the case of the United States and other open-access societies is the creation of an institutional structure that maximizes trials and eliminates errors and, therefore, maximizes the potential for achieving a successful outcome.

He's trying. No puzzling terms of art. Trying, but he has lost touch with common prose. The passage *seems to* speak plainly but gets fuzzier the more you ponder it. It repays analysis. Let's take our usual PM path into the first sentence.

The perpetuation
of open-access societies
like the United States
in a world
of continuous novel change
raises a fundamental institutional dilemma
at the heart
of the issue
of economic development and
of successful dynamic change.

Remember my earlier alert against three "of"s in a row? A sure sign of sleep-writing. Here is the classic Official Style pattern: prepositional-phrase string plus statement + prepositional-phrase string. So we know that the shape of the sentence *by itself* invokes blur and boredom. Hard to know just *exactly* what is being said in all those nouns: perpetuation, open-access societies, world, continuous novel change, institutional dilemma, heart, issue, economic development, dynamic change. What relationship do they bear to one another, *exactly*? Let's start, as the PM recommends, by trying to get rid of some prepositional phrases. What about "a world of continuous novel change"? Is there any kind of "change" that is not "novel"? Can we get away with the common cliché "changing world"? I don't see why not. And "open-access societies" is another cliché in fancy dress: "open society." Do we need "the perpetuation of"? If we just said "Open societies like the United States in a changing world . . . ," wouldn't that cover the ground? I don't quite see how "perpetuation" of something "raises a fundamental institutional dilemma" so let's bypass it for now and continue on to "at the heart of the issue of economic development and of successful dynamic change." We can condense "the issue of economic development" to "economic development." And what does "successful dynamic change" mean here? In this context, it can only mean "economic development," so far as I can see. So, thus far:

> Open societies like the United States in a changing world raise a fundamental institutional dilemma at the heart of economic development.

Next sentence.

> By uncertainty we mean that we do not know what is going to happen in the future...

STOP RIGHT HERE. DUH! By uncertainty we mean uncertainty. Ah, yes. And the rest of the sentence:

> And that condition [that is, uncertainty] characterizes the world we have been creating.

An uncertain world is characterized by uncertainty. That is, "We live in an uncertain world." Aha! Another cliché. Followed by another: "How can our minds make sense of new and novel conditions?" Don't "new" and "novel" mean the same thing? "How do we make sense of novelty?" Can't we just say "We live in an uncertain, puzzling world"? Or, if you want a question, "How can we make sense of this uncertain world we have created?" I don't see why not. If I've missed something, figure out what it is.

The revision so far:

> Open societies like the United States in a changing world raise a fundamental institutional dilemma at the heart of economic development. How can we make sense of this uncertain world we have created?

So the "fundamental institutional dilemma" must mean that open societies create a continuously changing world that is hard to understand. Why not just say this, and junk the "fundamental institutional dilemma" blah blah blah?

> Open societies create a continuously changing world that is hard to understand. How do we understand it?

Next and last sentence:

> The answer that **in** fact has proven successful **in** the case **of** the United States and other open-access societies **is** the creation **of** an institutional structure that maximizes trials and eliminates errors and, therefore, maximizes the potential **for** achieving a successful outcome.

This sentence answers the "How do we understand it?" question. Some of this sentence is pure Official Style guff: "maximizes the potential for achieving a successful outcome"; "institutional structure" for "institution." And "maximizes trials and eliminates errors" is our old friend the cliché "trial and error." So we have:

> Open societies answer this question by creating institutions that work through trial and error.

So, a final revision:

> Open societies create a continuously changing world that is hard to understand. How do we understand it? Open societies answer this question by creating institutions that work through trial and error.

But wait a minute. Do we really need "that is hard to understand"? Isn't it implied by "How do we understand it"? Or can't we, at least, get away with adding "puzzling" after "continuously changing"? So a final final revision:

> Open societies create a puzzling, continuously changing world. How do we understand it? Open societies answer this question by creating institutions that work through trial and error. (27 words)

And here's the original again:

> The perpetuation of open-access societies like the United States in a world of continuous novel change raises a fundamental institutional dilemma at the heart of the issue of economic development and of successful dynamic change. By uncertainty, we mean that we do not know what is going to happen in the future, and that condition characterizes the world we have been creating. How can our minds make sense of new and novel conditions? The answer that in fact has proven successful in the case of the United States and other open-access societies is the creation of an institutional structure that maximizes trials and eliminates errors and, therefore, maximizes the potential for achieving a successful outcome. (115 words)

Our long—and yes, I know, tedious—analysis has found beneath the stupendissimo lard factor of 77% only a collection of banal clichés. In the plain language translation, the banality shows. Professional languages usually cover it up. The perfect illustration of a primary danger: the illusion that communication has occurred when it hasn't. A string of tautological clichés pretending to be wisdom. Why couldn't the writer see it? Why couldn't the editors at the *Wall Street Journal* see it and refuse to publish the piece? Muddled banalities don't really interpret, they only seem to.

But wait! Maybe an economist would find this op-ed piece easier going. As it happens, I discussed it with a group of economists. Their verdict? "He doesn't say anything. What are they doing publishing stuff like that?"

WARREN BUFFETT REVISES

When you translate from a professional language into plain English, you are always afraid you may miss some vital argument that requires the special language. This fear keeps us away, most of all, from legal language. Here's an example of a pro taking on the legal language. Warren Buffett, the most famous investor in America, was once set an Official Style revision exercise very like the ones we have been pursuing. He was asked to translate a fund prospectus into plain English. He should know, if anyone does, when a special language is required.

Original:

Maturity and Duration Management

Maturity and duration management decisions are made in the context of an intermediate maturity orientation. The maturity structure of the portfolio is adjusted in anticipation of cyclical interest rate changes. Such adjustments are not made in an effort to capture short-term, day-to-day movements in the market, but instead are implemented in anticipation of longer term, secular shifts in the levels of interest rates (i.e. shifts transcending and/or not inherent in the business cycle). Adjustments made to shorten portfolio maturity and duration are made to limit capital losses during periods when interest rates are expected to rise. Conversely, adjustments made to lengthen maturation for the portfolio's maturity and duration strategy lie in analysis of the U.S. and global economies, focusing on levels of real interest rates, monetary and fiscal policy actions, and cyclical indicators. [133 words]

Buffett's revision:

We will try to profit by correctly predicting future interest rates. When we have no strong opinion, we will generally hold intermediate term bonds. But when we expect a major and sustained increase in rates, we will concentrate on short-term issues. And, conversely, if we expect a major shift to lower rates, we will buy long bonds. We will focus on the big picture and won't make moves based on short-term considerations. [72 words] (*USA Today*, 14 Oct. 1994)

Buffett is obviously our kind of guy—a 46% lard factor and a clear statement dredged from a hopeless swamp. Not only that, but we can trust the dredger to know what the original means. Buffett on a fund prospectus is like sterling on silver. We are free to concentrate on how he did it.

Original:

Maturity and duration management decisions are made in the context of an intermediate maturity orientation. The maturity structure of the portfolio is adjusted in anticipation of cyclical interest rate changes.

Original visualized by PM Rules 1 and 2:
Maturity and duration management decisions
>   **are** made
>>   *in* the context
>>   *of* an intermediate maturity orientation.

The maturity structure
>>   *of* the portfolio
>   **is** adjusted
>>   *in* anticipation
>>   *of* cyclical interest rate changes.

OK. Standard Official Style formula:

- passive "no actor" verbs ("decisions are made")
- strings of prepositional phrases fore and aft
- lots of Latinate official-sounding words: maturity, duration, management, decisions, context, intermediate, orientation, etc.

What does Buffett do with it?

We will try to profit by correctly predicting future interest rates.

Huzzah! He tells us who is doing the deciding: "*We* will try to profit. . . ." That helps reduce the prepositional-phrase inventory from five to one. He makes clear the main action: "try to profit." This main *action* sticks close by the *actor*. The sentence *starts fast.* The first five rules of the PM, put into practice. And he tells us how *We* are going to do it: "predicting future interest rates." The lard factor on this segment—11 words for 30—is an awesome 63%. Onward.

Original:
Such adjustments are not made in an effort to capture short-term, day-to-day movements in the market, but instead are implemented in anticipation of longer term, secular shifts in the levels of interest rates (i.e. shifts transcending and/or not inherent in the business cycle).

Original as PM-diagrammed:

Such adjustments
> **are** not made
>> *in* an effort
>> *to* capture short-term, day-to-day movements
>> *in* the market,

but instead
> **are** implemented
>> *in* anticipation
>> *of* longer term, secular shifts
>> *in* the levels
>> *of* interest rates
>>> (i.e., shifts transcending and/or not inherent
>>> *in* the business cycle).

The mixture as before, but even more shapeless. How does Buffett decode it?

> When we have no strong opinion, we will generally hold intermediate term bonds.

Huzzah × 2!—LF 70%. Again, clear *actor* and *action*: "When we have ... we will ... hold." Plain words—"strong opinion," "generally hold"—instead of Latinate jawbreakers. And he has complied with the Lanham Act of Prepositional Phrase Reduction by eliminating all seven prepositional phrases. Now for stage three.

Original:

Adjustments made to shorten portfolio maturity and duration are made to limit capital losses during periods when interest rates are expected to rise.

Buffett translation:

But when we expect a major and sustained increase in rates, we will concentrate on short-term issues.

Now we detect a shape in Buffett's own prose. We'll align on the main *actor*.

We will try to profit by correctly predicting future interest rates.

When   **we have** no strong opinion,
    we will generally hold intermediate term bonds.

But when   **we expect** a major and sustained increase in rates,
    we will concentrate on short-term issues.

A financial prospectus should tell us how a prospective management intends to act. It represents interpretation at its most vital. It couldn't be better done than this. The prose takes on a clear *shape* that comes from its essential purpose. When A, we will do A+; when B, we will do B+. The rest of Buffett's revision follows this form.

And, conversely,

if   **we expect** a major shift to lower rates,
    we will buy long bonds.
    We will focus on the big picture and
    won't make moves based on short-term considerations.

Buffett does not present his prose diagrammatically patterned, but the pattern, the *shape* of the sentences, could scarcely be clearer. **We will** or **We won't**, depending on the circumstances. He does not shrink from a term of art like "long bond" (instead of "to lengthen maturation for the portfolio's maturity and duration strategy") when he needs one, but he does not need many and he doesn't use many. This goes for most professional languages. Nor does he shrink from a common expression when it does the job—"focus on the big picture," instead of "analysis of the U.S. and global economies."

Why, it is logical to ask after this analysis, was the original prospectus not written Buffett-style to begin with? The writer wanted to sound official, authoritative, *legal*. Buffett, with his investment track record, doesn't need to. Not for nothing have the annual reports Buffett writes for his company, Berkshire Hathaway, become classics. He is a master at interpreting his business for his stockholders.

THE LAWYERS

Now for another example of interpretive failure. The lawyers have long ruled the kingdom of long, shapeless sentences. Here is a typical one from a loan contract:

> In the event **Buyer defaults** on any payment, or fails to obtain or maintain the insurance required hereunder, or fails to comply with any other provision hereof, or a proceeding in bankruptcy, receivership or insolvency shall be instituted by or against Buyer or his property, or Seller deems the property in danger of misuse or confiscation, or Seller otherwise reasonably deems the indebtedness or the property insecure, **Seller shall have the right** to declare all amounts due or to become due hereunder to be immediately due and payable.

This sentence confuses the ordinary reader—perhaps its intent—by distending its shape. Between the opening "In the event" and the clause that completes this meaning, "Seller shall have the right . . . ," intervene a string of qualifications. We lose our way because we don't know what the qualifications apply to. The main utterance comes last instead of first, where it would orient us. I have exposed the sentence shape by a simple typographical modification.

The convention of consecutive prose obscures the shape of thought. On an electronic screen, we can now suspend that sometimes confusing convention and reshape for thought. Let's try it. I won't change the wording, only the order and the layout:

> Seller shall have the right to declare all amounts due or to become due hereunder to be immediately due and payable, in the event:
>
> 1. Buyer defaults on any payment, or fails to obtain or maintain the insurance required hereunder, or
> 2. fails to comply with any other provision hereof, or
> 3. a proceeding in bankruptcy, receivership or insolvency shall be instituted by or against Buyer or his property, or
> 4. Seller deems the property in danger of misuse or confiscation, or
> 5. Seller otherwise reasonably deems the indebtedness or the property insecure.

> Seller can declare all amounts immediately payable, if:
>
> 1. **Buyer** defaults on payment or insurance
> 2. **Buyer** fails to comply with any other provision
> 3. **Buyer** goes bankrupt
> 4. **Seller** deems the indebtedness or property in danger

Whether or not the *writer* uses such a presentation, the *reader* can now recreate it as necessary. Since I'm not an attorney, I don't know how my revision would stand at law. I have simply revised for *shape*, removing the formulaic repetition and using format and typography to help me understand what is being written.

Happily, we have a check on my revision. I took this example from an article on plain-language laws.[1] The authors give a legally sound translation, but one that I have not reviewed since I first read the article several years ago. I'll turn the page now and find out what their revision looks like:

> We can declare the full amount you owe us due any time we want to.

Aha! They have been more daring than I dared to be—but then, they have a right to be, they are lawyers. They have interpreted the law for the people who need to understand it. But even if we had been willing to desert the law library for the world of common sense, as they did, going through the revision we practiced would be the best way to do it. When you are revising, always proceed step by step. If you just junk the sentence and substitute a paraphrase of your own—as the lawyers did here—though that may finally be the best thing to do, you'll not learn *why* the prose defeated you.

Before leaving the language of the law, let's reverse our revision polarity with a couple of parodies. The first is by James

---

[1]"Plain-Language Laws: Giving the Consumer an Even Break," Michael Ferry and Richard B. Teitelman, *Clearinghouse Review*, Vol. 14, No. 6 (Oct. 1980), pp. 522ff.

B. Minor, "an attorney turned writer teacher," who tells us how a lawyer would say "Give us this day our daily bread."

> We respectfully petition, request and entreat that due and adequate provision be made, this day and the date hereinafter subscribed, for the satisfying of this petitioner's nutritional requirements and for the organizing of such methods as may be deemed necessary and proper to assure the reception by and for said petitioner of such quantities of baked cereal products as shall, in the judgment of the aforesaid petitioner, constitute a sufficient supply thereof.[2]

And here's a plain-language version of the software disclaimer we all click the "Agreed" button for, this from Haventree Software.

> If EasyFlow doesn't work: tough. If you lose millions because EasyFlow messes up, it's you that's out the millions, not us. If you don't like this disclaimer: tough. We reserve the right to do the absolute minimum provided by law, up to and including nothing. This is basically the same disclaimer that comes with all software packages, but ours is in plain English and theirs is in legalese. We didn't want to include any disclaimer at all, but our lawyers insisted. (*Wired*, January 1994)

A MISSION STATEMENT

Interpretive bureaucracies often seek to explain themselves to the outside world in a now-classic genre, the "mission statement." Here, by definition, the professional bureaucracy must preach to the outside world and not just to the choir. It must justify its existence by explaining its activities in a way the ordinary person can understand. If it speaks only to itself, and in a language only it can understand, it loses its reason for being.

---

[2]Ronald L. Goldfarb and James C. Raymond, *Clear Understandings* (New York: Random House, 1982) p. 6.

Here's a mission statement for a field of study—"augmented cognition"—which has recently become large enough to create its own bureaucracy. Augmented cognition studies the ways in which computers can be used to enhance human thinking in warfare. Since computers play so large a part in battle nowadays, using them to increase the speed and accuracy of human response under stress has become an important part of military planning. Thus the field researches what is commonly called the "HCI," or human-computer interface. The people who do this research must explain themselves both to their immediate paymasters, the military who support their research, and more largely to the citizens who finally pay for it. This field has come to be known by the clunky if obvious abbreviation "Aug Cog." (If only "aug" rhymed with "cog" or vice versa, it would fly under a nicer-sounding nickname.) Here's how Aug Cog explains itself to the rest of us who pay the bills.

> The mission of Aug Cog is to extend, by an order or magnitude or more, the information management capacity of the human-computer warfighting integral by developing and demonstrating quantifiable enhancements to human cognitive ability in diverse, stressful, operational environments. Specifically, this program will empower one human's ability to successfully accomplish the functions currently carried out by three or more individuals.
>
> A key objective of the program is to foster development of novel—and improvement of identifiable—prototypes and enabling technologies, in order to experiment with and understand the means by which they may be integrated into existing operational systems, as well as those in development. The program will accomplish this by delivering new design principles for human-computer symbiosis.
>
> The Augmented Cognition program will explore the interaction of cognitive, perceptual, neurological, and digital domains to develop improved performance application concepts. The advanced applications will be tailored to military problems in order to demonstrate potential pay-off for operational users. Success will improve the way 21st Century warriors interact with computer based systems, advance systems design methodologies, and fundamentally re-engineer military decision making.

Don't worry. We won't be revising the whole thing. I just wanted you to see the full context. Here's the first sentence. It is a toughie. (They are all toughies, actually. Try your hand at revising one.) As usual, a PM diagram helps us get our bearings.

The mission
of Aug Cog
is
to extend,
by an order
of magnitude or more, the information management capacity
of the human-computer warfighting integral
by developing and demonstrating quantifiable enhancements
to human cognitive ability
in diverse, stressful, operational environments.

OK. Who's the main actor? "Aug Cog." What is Aug Cog doing? "Extending." What is it extending? "information management capacity." Whose, what's, "Information management capacity"? Well, "the human-computer warfighting integral." Here we stumble over the sentence's main problem. What does this phrase mean? I guess it means the combination of human and computer as this combination is used in warfare. "Integral" in ordinary language is an adjective that means "necessary for completeness." That doesn't really fit here. There is a noun "integral" used in mathematics; it means the solution of a differential equation. That doesn't seem to work here, either. And is "extend" what you do to "information management capacity? Don't you *expand* it? Or *improve* it? Or *enrich* it? Anyway, the root idea seems to be this: "Aug Cog aims to speed up how humans use computers to manage information in war." Or maybe (since "war" may be too specific a term): "Aug Cog aims to speed up how human-computer combinations manage information under stress." Not elegant but the best I can do.

Now for the second half of the sentence:

by developing and demonstrating quantifiable enhancements
to human cognitive ability
in diverse, stressful, operational environments.

Obviously, we need a new sentence for this, since stuffing it into one bewilders us with the flood of adjective-noun general terms. The Aug Cog folks think they can speed up this information processing by "an order of magnitude." What's that, you ask? It means, "by ten times." Oh. But they haven't done it yet. That's what they hope to do. So let's be honest: "We hope that our research can show how to make the information flow ten times faster than it does now and do it in ways we can measure." So we have a revision that looks like this.

> Aug Cog aims to speed up how human-computer combinations manage information under stress. We hope that our research will show how to make information flow ten times as fast as it does now and do it in ways we can measure.

Or maybe:

> Aug Cog studies how computers can be used to make people think and communicate faster under the stresses of war. Ten times faster, we hope.

Now for the second sentence. Original again:

> Specifically, this program will empower one human's ability to successfully accomplish the functions currently carried out by three or more individuals.

An easy one.

> One person will do the work of three.

So we have a final revision:

> Aug Cog studies how computers can be used to make people think and communicate faster under the stresses of war. Ten times faster, we hope. One person will do the work of three. (LF 45%)

I'm not happy with this revision, but it's the best I can come up with. I will leave the second and third paragraphs up to you, and stop with a general reflection. What the Aug Cog people are really studying is how to use computers to make people think better and quicker. They are trying to augment human cognition using computers. But the military is paying the bills, so the research has to be about improving our thinking in the various battles we'll have to fight in the future. The main purpose can't go in the prospectus. The prospectus certainly can be made clearer, but it needs a Warren Buffett to do it.

This passage was given to me by somebody working in the Aug Cog world when I asked what goes on there. Here, I was told, is the explanation for the outside world; read and understand. As an explanation for the outside world, the mission statement is a fiasco. About communication, their subject, they know from nothing. It is a damning revelation.

A Salutary Tale

The modern American university has accumulated a hodgepodge of professional languages, each spoken in its own disciplinary bureaucracy. All goes well—or seems to—so long as each group stays in its own bureau, but things can go badly wrong when they try to talk to each other about a subject of common interest like, for example, the digital communication system that connects them. (Students are a different story; they must pass from one bureaucratic language to another every day, but their professors don't know—or care—about that.)

Here follows a story about such an effort at a university with which I am familiar. A panel of distinguished visiting IT (information technology) experts examined the campus information system and submitted a report. The report, written in the IT dialect of the Official Style, was not readily understood by the people for whom it was intended, the faculty. A fuss followed. To factor out how much of the fuss was caused by the recommendations, and how much by the language in which they were couched, would require much more space than we have here. (A lot could be learned from such a study, supplying as it does a pattern-case of

Official Style misunderstandings.) To orient us, let's begin with a plain-language summary of the report by someone intimately acquainted with its subject.

> UXXX uses a lot of incompatible information systems that can't talk to each other, or to the outside world. Neither can the people who use them. Some parts of the present configuration should be preserved but most of them should be changed to a centralized system.

Major changes were to come from the report, and the chairperson of the academic senate urged the faculty to read it.

> I encourage you to read the entire report and to provide comment on it in its entirety.

That is, "Please read the report carefully and comment on it." OK. Let's see what we see. The letter accompanying the report gives a hint of what is to follow. Look at the first two sentences.

> Attached is the final report of the external IT/Networking review panel. It reflects the unanimous views of the reviewers.

For a start, the second sentence can be condensed into a single adjective, "unanimous," thus eliminating the "views" of the "reviewers" repetition. And if we move "external" over we get rid of the ambiguity about whether the panel is external or the IT/Networking.

> Attached is the final, and unanimous, report of the IT/Networking external review panel.

Nit-picking? Well, maybe, though we've saved one third of the reader's time. Try another sentence.

> UXXX has exceptional strength in the many extraordinary skilled and knowledgeable IT people we found across the campus and in the unusual level of resources committed to departmentalized IT support. (30 words)

"Resources" is the accepted Official Style euphemism for money. And we need to clarify what "departmentalized" means, because that turns out to be the crux of the report's criticism.

> UXXX has many skilled IT people and spends a lot of money on IT support for individual departments. (18 words; LF 40%)

Here's what it says about departmental support in the report.

Original:
Compared to most of its peers, UXXX has made, and continues to make, an atypically heavy investment in localized IT support and equipment. (23 words)

Revision:
UXXX spends more money on localized IT support and equipment than most of its peers. (15 words; LF 35%)

And this investment makes people happy:

> This has resulted in a very rich level of responsiveness to departmental needs and desires. The review team is not in a position to do a cost/benefit evaluation of this level of investment, but it seems clear that it enables an unusually vibrant and responsive departmental academic and clinical IT environment that admirably energizes departmental endeavors and serves academic needs. (61 words)

Most of this is pure Official Style guff. How about this revision?

> And this investment pays off. Departmental needs are very well served. (11 words; LF 82%)

Have I left out anything essential? I don't think so. The passage is full of impressionistic description ("very rich level of responsiveness" and "vibrant and responsive departmental academic and clinical IT environment") and needless repetition ("admirably energizes departmental endeavors and serves academic needs"). A lard factor of 82% would astonish us in any context but here it is fatal. "Look. Money is short," a careful reader of the report would reason. "These guys seem to be recommending that we create a centralized system. Don't tell me it won't come at the expense of the support I need in my department." Departmental computer support lay at the heart of the controversy. The faculty felt that this report recommended taking away their local computer support and putting it back in the centralized office where it used to be. A clear statement about this support would have defined the issue. Lathering on the guff only made it worse.

On to the heart of the report. This passage gives the full flavor of it.

> On the *networking* front UXXX has a challenging degree of combinatorial complexity with many diverging approaches. In general, UXXX has a network infrastructure that is significantly at variance from most of its peer institutions. This degree of divergence from the mainstream of networking will be of particular importance in the future where, as an outlier facing inexorably changing network and middle-ware infrastructure largely alone, UXXX will not likely be able to leverage much in the way of the technology, architecture or business approaches.

We can now see the center of the report's style: laudatory guff on the one hand, opaque technical terminology on the other.

Let's pick out two of the buzzwords that run through the report, and give them the attention the academic senate chairperson recommended.

Infrastructure. This has become a, maybe *the*, central buzzword for dialects across the Official Style. It is the central term of art in this report. What does it mean? Let's start with an excerpt from the online *Wikipedia* entry for the word.

> **Infrastructure** is the set of interconnected structural elements that provide the framework for supporting the entire structure. The term is often used very abstractly. For instance, software engineering tools are sometimes described as part of the infrastructure of a development shop, and the term infrastructural capital in economics may be overly broad, as it includes a range from clothing to a continent-spanning canal system.

Aha! "Often used very abstractly." It can refer to roads, railroads, bridges, public services. A qualified definition narrows it down to what the report is talking about:

> Infrastructure means fixed equipment and installations, including widely deployed software. For example, computers, cables, wireless routers, network hubs, mail servers (including the server software), web servers (including the web server software), can all be subsumed under the genus, infrastructure. Intelligent people are not part of the infrastructure.

If you were writing for an audience outside the field, wouldn't it help to specify what "infrastructure" means?

Leverage is a second popular buzzword, as in "UXXX will not likely be able to leverage much in the way of the technology, architecture or business approaches." The first dictionary meaning is "the action of a lever." Use a crowbar to open a stuck door. Obviously, "leverage" as a buzzword has left this meaning behind. Second meaning: "positional advantage, power to act effectively." Third meaning: "use of credit to improve one's speculative capacity." Buying a stock on margin is this kind of leverage. The kind we want must be the second meaning: "positional advantage."

Now, back to the passage. Don't lose patience. It will be the last one we'll analyze. First sentence.

> On the *networking* front UXXX has a challenging degree of combinatorial complexity with many diverging approaches.

"On the *networking* front" must mean "networks," no? What else could it mean? And "challenging degree of combinatorial complexity with many diverging approaches." Well, what *specifically* can this mean? I don't know, so I'll guess.

> UXXX networks are complex and intricately connected.

And what about "In general, UXXX has a network infrastructure that is significantly at variance from most of its peer institutions."

What does "infrastructure" mean here? I thought at first that it meant the complex pattern of networks. But now we have a definition to plug in.

> Infrastructure means fixed equipment and installations, including widely deployed software. For example, computers, cables, wireless routers, network hubs, mail servers (including the server software), web servers (including the web server software), can all be subsumed under the genus, infrastructure.

So the "networking front" may, in fact probably does, include not only the networks but the software and fixed equipment. But do not these, together, *constitute* the network? I don't know. I am a targeted reader for the report and this confusion was, for me, fundamental. Much easier to revise the sentence than to really understand it.

Original:
In general, UXXX has a network infrastructure that is significantly at variance from most of its peer institutions.

Revision:
UXXX's network infrastructure differs from that of peer institutions.

Now we've reached the last sentence! Maybe we can use it to leverage our comprehension of the infrastructure of the networking front.

> This degree of divergence from the mainstream of networking will be of particular importance in the future where, as an outlier facing inexorably changing network and middle-ware infrastructure largely alone, UXXX will not likely be able to leverage much in the way of the technology, architecture or business approaches.

Start at the end. What does "UXXX will not likely be able to leverage much in the way of the technology, architecture or business approaches" mean? The whole report is full of mealy-mouthed qualifications like "degree of divergence," "not likely" and "leverage much," so we can get rid of them. We confront: "UXXX will not be able to leverage the technology, architecture or business approaches." "Technology" and "business approaches" are very general words, "business approaches" so general as to be meaningless. "Architecture" as in "computer architecture" is, I think, a term of art, with a specific meaning. But in this list, who knows? We know what "leverage" as a verb means, however: "power to act effectively." "UXXX will not be able act effectively on the technology, architecture, or business approaches." Huh?

Back to the first part of the sentence.

> This degree of divergence from the mainstream of networking will be of particular importance in the future where, as an outlier facing inexorably changing network and middle-ware infrastructure largely alone, . . .

Is "middle-ware infrastructure" different from the earlier "network infrastructure"? Seems so, by the grammatical construction of it: "inexorably changing network and middle-ware infrastructure." So we have two "infrastructures" (refer back to our earlier definition if you are confused). They differ from those used at other places. As hardware and software change in those places, UXXX, alone and disconnected, won't be able to use them. That, at least, is my best guess at the meaning.

As I've said so often before in this book, we're not talking here about small mistakes and stylistic inelegancies. We're talking about a major, and in this case *really* major, failure to communicate. And to communicate *about a communication system*. You can see here so clearly how a dependence on buzzwords and tacit understandings about their meaning fool the writers into thinking that they have communicated to the audience they are addressing. And, with equal clarity, you can see how the buzzwords fool the writers into thinking that they have been thinking. Instead: "leverage much in the way of the technology, architecture or business approaches." No wonder their report caused a furor.

Interpretive bureaucracies must interpret, explain complex problems in ways that the rest of us can understand. As in the mission statement considered earlier, so in this report to a faculty by an outside committee, *the genre itself requires that complex material must be made comprehensible to an outside audience.* It didn't happen here.

Again: Explaining what you do to outsiders is no longer a peripheral activity for a professional bureaucracy. Professional bureaucracies have become interpretive bureaucracies and explaining what they do is fundamental to their being. Fail in it and you have failed your own profession, the professions that surround it, and, worst of all, the people who pay the bills. And, sooner or later, those failures will come back to haunt you.

CHAPTER

7

Electronic Prose

When you display written words on an electronic screen rather than imprint them on paper, reading itself changes radically; electronic "literacy" turns out to differ in fundamental ways from "print" literacy. And electronic literacy increasingly dominates the workplace. Anyone working in present-day America confronts these radical changes in expressive medium, in "literacy," in reading and writing, every day. Even a practical, hands-on guide like *Revising Prose* must pause to reflect on these changes, for they have transformed how the written word lives and works in human life.

Changes close to home first. We have already noticed how word processors enhance prose revision. They make it much easier not only to get the words "down" (though "on screen" rather than "on paper") but also to take them up and move them around. And the speed with which revision takes place means, often, that more revision can take place when writing—as we usually do—under a deadline. No need to go through those one-day retyping turnarounds for each revision that pre-computer writers remember so well. And electronic spelling and grammar checkers and the electronic thesaurus, by speeding up ordinary procedures, further encourage revision. Global searches can find prepositional-phrase strings and tell you if every main verb is "is." Use global search-and-replace to put a return at the end of each sentence for a page or two and you'll get a pretty good idea of sentence-length variation. Word counters make computing the lard factor much faster. The malign hand of buzzwords emerges clearly from the parodic web programs that combine them at random. And changes in layout and typography become a handy analytical tool to find one's way in the Official Style's pathless prose woods. Because the computer is a rule-based device, it lends itself to a rule-based revision method. All in all, prose paramedics have never had it so easy.

VISUALIZATION AND VOICING

But digital text has changed literacy more profoundly than these helpful easements suggest. Most important, the relationship between verbal and visual communication is changing. Images more and more both supplement and replace written information. For statistical presentation of all sorts, old-fashioned pie charts and bar graphs have given way to more imaginative and three-dimensional renderings. Even simple spreadsheet programs encourage the visualization of numeric data, and computer graphics now routinely model all kinds of complex dynamic processes in three dimensions and real time.

We are so used to the convention of print—linear, regular left-to-right and top-to-bottom, black-and-white, constant font and type size—that we have forgotten how constraining it is. Black-and-white print is remarkable for its power to express conceptual thought, but equally remarkable for all the powers it renounces in doing so. No pictures, no color, no perspective. Until recently these things have been just too expensive. No longer. On the electronic screen, you can do them all and a lot more. And as electronic memory gets ever cheaper, they have come within the reach of everyday wordsmiths as well as graphic designers.

The constraints of conventionally printed prose are slowly dissolving. If we can use color, font size and shape, three-dimensional effects like drop-shadow and the like, then we will use them. If we can intersperse text and graphics with ease, we'll come to depend on the combination. All these changes, in their turn, are changing how we write and indeed how we think. It is no exaggeration to say that electronic textual information has now become three dimensional. The black-and-white, letters-only convention concentrates on abstract thought—the "meaning"—to the exclusion of everything else. Tonal colorations there will always be—they are what we usually call "style"—but in print they work always beneath the surface, implicit rather than explicit. Bringing them to the surface takes time and trouble. With the electronic word, however, these tonal colorations can be explicit rather than implicit. We will be able, literally, to "color" our communications with one another. And there will be no going back, no abjuration of this new realm of communication. If you can write "in color," and choose not to, that too will be a "communication," and usually one you will not want to make.

What do these changes imply for literacy in the workplace and the schools and colleges that prepare students for it? Well, for a start, they dramatize a need I have been advocating all through this book, a need to use the visual imagination in reading, writing, and revising. More than ever, we must notice the shape of prose. Up to now, "graphics" people tended to work in one office and "word" people in another. No more. From now on, graphics will be part of a writer's basic training. Words and images are now inextricably intertwined in our common expressive repertoire.

The desktop-publishing revolution reinforces this change at every point. Typography and layout, once a special field, in electronic displays become an expressive parameter for all writers. Type fonts have become *allegorical*, able to invoke a particular mood, represent an attitude, speak as pictures as well as symbols. The classic creed of the typographer has always been that the written surface should be transparent—never noticed for itself, serving only the meaning shining through its lucid waters. That theory needs adjustment. We will be looking *at* the prose surface as much as looking *through* it. And that is what *Revising Prose* has always had in mind. Revision means exactly this oscillation between looking *at* and looking *through* a prose surface. The natural logic of electronic text leads more naturally to this *at/through* oscillation than does print, and so invites revision in a way fixed print does not.

I've also been arguing that prose—now universally read in silence—should be *voiced*, at least in the auditory imagination. Rule 6 of the PM: Read the passage aloud. The digitized word reinforces and empowers this recommendation as well, since we can now talk to the computer and it can talk back. Before long, voicing will be a routine dimension of the electronic word. We will move from voice to writing to image and back again in ways new to human expression. The Official Style pushes prose to its voiceless extreme. We have seen that over and over; *read it aloud* and the Official Style sounds silly, absurdly pompous, often simply pointless. Voice is now returning to writing in ways so structural as to recall an oral culture rather than a written one. *Voiceless* prose won't work much longer.

MULTIMEDIA PROSE

All these changes have come together in an emergent job category—the information designer, a person who fits the information to the expressive medium. At the core of the computer revolution stands a polyvalent code, a set of symbols that can be expressed by words, images, or sound. The different parts of the human sensorium now share a common digital code. Obviously, we will not usually want to express the information on a hospital chart in musical form (although it has been done). But information itself is now *designed*. The information designer orchestrates modes of expression. Writing prose has become part of a larger endeavor that must decide first *how the information will be expressed*: through word, image, sound, or a mixture of the three. Plato dreamed of such a union, hoping to find the common focus for all knowledge in mathematics. In more than a manner of speaking, that dream has come true.

Electronic literacy, then, differs markedly from print literacy. It knows how to mix alphabetic information with information coming from image and sound. People at every level communicate in a richer but more complex informational sensorium. Writing has come to mean something different, and writers who don't know, and feel, this will find themselves the clerks of a forgotten mood.

Prose style, in the world of the conventional printed book, works in a carefully protected vacuum. Extraneous signals are carefully filtered out. Typography and layout aim to help us concentrate on textual meaning without distracting our attention to themselves. Writers are people who are good with words. Pictures and sounds only distract them. This isolation has encouraged and reinforced the Official Style. It could be unreadable because nobody ever listened to it read aloud. It could be shapeless because nobody ever looked at its shape. Multimedia prose encourages us to look and listen.

VOLATILE TEXT AND TEXTUAL AUTHORITY

Other constitutional changes come with the electronic word. Perhaps foremost, *authority* diffuses itself between writer and reader. Although we seldom think of it in this way, the print medium is fundamentally authoritarian. "In print" means unchangeable. You can't quarrel with it. This penumbra of authority goes back a long way. The Renaissance humanists resurrected the authority of classical Greek and Latin culture by editing that culture's documents into fixed printed texts. The authoritative edition means the unchanging edition, text fixed forever, a lodestone of cultural authority. We still feel that way about print. It *fixes* things.

Electronic text *unfixes* them. It is by nature changeable, antiauthoritarian. If we don't like what it says, we can change it, ornament it, revise it, erase it, mock it in letters indistinguishable from the original ones. Patterns of authority have shifted, become democratized. This democratization means that the electronic word will mean something quite different from the printed one. Anyone interested in writing of any sort must understand this change.

It operates, for a start, upon the role the writer adopts as a writer. When we write we inevitably adopt a social role of some sort. Trying to bring this presentation of self to self-consciousness has been one of our main tasks in this book. Surely all of us have noticed that the self we adopt in computer communication, especially on-line and, to a lesser degree in e-mail, differs from our "print" self. For reasons I leave to the psychologists, computers have from their beginnings evoked the game and play ranges of human motivation far more strongly than print has. "Hacker," before it became a synonym for computer vandal, used to be an innocent word, used to describe kids who liked to play around with computers just for the fun of it, do something just to see if it could be done. This original hacker mentality inevitably creeps in whenever we put our fingers on the computer's home row: We hold language more lightly in our hands; our sense of humor stands closer; we can't take things, or ourselves, so seriously.

A good predisposition this turns out to be—returning from theory to home concerns—for avoiding the Official Style and its systematic pomposity. The "dignity of print" has a lot to answer for. Let's hope that the electronic word preserves the muse of comedy that has hovered around its creation. Blog prose seems to suggest that it has. At all events, it is something to be alert to if you are writing and revising prose in an electronic world. It has created a new communications decorum.

ALLEGORICAL ALPHABETS

This book is not the place to illustrate the changes electronic text brings with it. In the first place, no book can: The printed book is just what electronic text is transcending. In the second place, *Revising Prose* is a hands-on guide, not a theoretical discussion. But perhaps an example or two can sketch the revolution in typography that the personal computer is bringing about.

The printed book, as we have known it since Gutenberg, depends on print as essentially transparent and unself-conscious. We do not notice it as print. The book may be well designed or ill, and we may register that. But the type selected—the size and shape of the letters, the white space between and around them—does not form part of the meaning. Making all these selections, "speccing type" as the editors call it, is an editing and production task, not an authorial affair.

All this is changing. Typography can now be—and increasingly will become—allegorical, part of the meaning, an authorial not an editing function. This will allow us to *see* prose characteristics that formerly we could only talk about. We will be able to analyze and revise prose in new ways, using new mixtures of alphabet and icon. We can grasp how this process might work by using the font and graphics capabilities available on any graphics-capable monitor.

Here is a typical academic sentence:

> The integration of a set of common value patterns with the internalized need-disposition structure of the constituent personalities is the core phenomenon of the dynamics of social systems.

Huh? The usual shapeless shopping bag of general concepts held together by "is" and prepositional glue. Let's consider three diagrams of its structure, diagrams anyone can construct on a personal computer.

> The integration
> **of** a set
> **of** common value patterns
> **with** the internalized need-disposition structure
> **of** the constituent personalities
> *is* the core phenomenon
> **of** the dynamics
> **of** social systems.

The	**integration** of a set
of	**common value patterns**
with the	**internalized need-disposition structure**
of the	**constituent personalities**
is the	**core phenomenon**

of the	**dynamics**	
of	**social systems.**	

The		**integration** of a set
of	**common value**	**patterns**
with the	**inter. need-disp.**	**structure**
of the	**constituent**	**personalities**
is the	**core**	**phenomenon**
of the		**dynamics**
of	**social**	**systems**.

In the first, I have done one of our usual vertical preposition charts, but with a little enhancement to render the pattern more graphic.

The second diagram tries to plot what relationship the general terms bear to one another by listing them separately from the prepositions that glue them together in a string. The separate listing shows you immediately what is wrong: The concepts in the list bear no discernible relationship to one another. Nothing in the concepts themselves tells us how they might be related; the pressures for connection fall entirely on the prepositions. They cannot bear it. Their breakdown is what makes the passage so hard to read. And the qualification of the key terms by adjectives, which themselves represent key terms—"common value patterns," "internalized need-disposition structure," "constituent personalities"—makes things still worse.

So I rearranged the sentence into the third diagram, trying to set off the key words and indicate graphically the three basic levels that compose the sentence. The lack of any genuine relationship, causal or otherwise, between the central words in the right column shows up even more. You can, given the syntax of the sentence, rearrange the central terms several different ways and still make sense of a sort. Try it.

Diagrams like this provide a powerful analytical tool. You needn't sit there cudgeling your brains in paralytic silence. You can start trying to make sense of things right on the screen, using your eyes and hands to help you think. The need to "spec type" stimulates you to explore how the sentence fits together. And you can, by type selection, both display your analysis and demonstrate your attitude toward it.

Now a simpler sentence altogether: "These ideas create a frame for the paragraph." A series of typographical manipulations shows the stages of perception that follow from applying Rules 3 and 4 of the PM—finding the action and putting it in a single, simple verb.

These ideas **create a frame for** the paragraph.

These ideas create a frame for the paragraph.

These ideas **frame** the paragraph.

These ideas frame the paragraph.

I used an outline effect to echo the "framing" action of the sentence. This kind of punning comment is but one of many available when type selection can be an authorial rather than an editorial function.

In the next example, I changed type to show where, in midsentence, the reader gets lost. The second type selection tries to depict this confusion visually.

ORDINARY TYPOGRAPHY

However, consciousness does exist and it stimulates an antagonistic relationship between the acceptance of the role of self-consciousness and the disregard of the knowledge which is indigenous to consciousness for the adaptation of a more sentimental role.

ALLEGORICAL TYPOGRAPHY

However, consciousness does exist and it stimulates an antagonistic relationship between the acceptance of the role of self-consciousness and the ***disregard of the knowledge which is indigenous to consciousness for the adaptation of a more sentimental role.***

You can use a similar technique to spotlight a persistent sound-clash pattern, here a hissing "s," "sh," and "t" in the prose of a biologist whose prose remains persistently tone-deaf:

*S*in*ce* Darwin ini*ti*ally provided the means of *test*ing for the exi*ste*nce of an evolu*ti*onary pro*ce*ss and for *it*s *si*gnifican*ce* in accoun*ting* for the a*ttribu*tes of living organ*isms*, biolog*is*ts have accep*ted* with increa*sing* de*cis*iveness the hypo*thesis* tha*t* all a*ttribu*tes of life are ou*t*comes of tha*t simp*le pro*cess.*

In the next example, also written by a professor, I've tried to portray graphically the shapeless, unfocused prose by printing the passage three times, in typefaces that become progressively easier to read. The first makes us look at the shape of the sentence only, since it is so hard to read the typeface. We have to look *at* rather than *through* it. The second is easier, the third easier still. It yields, in turn, to our usual graph of the shopping-bag sentence; there I've tried to satirize the wallboard monotony by making the prepositions huge.

It is one of the paradoxes of the history of rhetoric that what was in Antiquity essentially an oral discipline for the pleading of law cases should have become in the Middle Ages in one of its major aspects, a written discipline for the drawing up of quasi-legal documents.

It is one of the paradoxes of the history of rhetoric that what was in Antiquity essentially an oral discipline for the pleading of law cases should have become in the Middle Ages in one of its major aspects, a written discipline for the drawing up of quasi-legal documents.

It is one of the paradoxes of the history of rhetoric that what was in Antiquity essentially an oral discipline for the pleading of law cases should have become in the Middle Ages in one of its major aspects, a written discipline for the drawing up of quasi-legal documents.

It **is** one
of the paradoxes
of the history
of rhetoric that what was
in antiquity essentially an oral discipline
for the pleading of law cases should have become
in the Middle Ages
in one
of its major aspects, a written discipline
for the drawing up
of quasi-legal documents.

Shall we try a revision of this sentence just for the heck of it? Why not? Here's the original again in plain type:

> It is one of the paradoxes of the history of rhetoric that what was in Antiquity essentially an oral discipline for the pleading of law cases should have become in the Middle Ages in one of its major aspects, a written discipline for the drawing up of quasi-legal documents. (49 words)

Academic writing perpetually qualifies its assertions, lest the writer be thought to generalize beyond her information. In the revision, I've dared to generalize. That, plus subtracting the dead-rocket opening and bleeping some prepositions, does the trick.

> ~~It is one of the paradoxes of the history of rhetoric that~~ what was in Antiquity ~~essentially~~ an oral discipline for ~~the~~ pleading ~~of~~ law cases should have become in the Middle Ages ~~in one of its major aspects,~~ a written discipline for ~~the~~ drawing up ~~of~~ quasi-legal documents.

So, finally:

> What was in Antiquity an oral discipline for pleading law cases became in the Middle Ages, paradoxically, a written discipline for drawing up quasi-legal documents. (25 words; LF 49%)

Not too bad. Our lard factor is right on the money and we've foregrounded the natural contrast of the argument—oral discipline vs. written discipline. We've sacrificed some qualification (e.g., "in one of its major aspects") but writing always involves such tradeoffs. The tradeoff is worth it here. And the writer risks no misunderstandings. Of course she is generalizing; how else do you get from Antiquity to the Middle Ages in a single sentence?

One difficulty remains unsurmounted, of course. My faithful *Webster's New Collegiate* defines "paradox" as: (1) "a tenet contrary to received opinion," (2) "an assertion seemingly opposed to common sense," (3) "a statement actually self-contradictory." The movement from oral to written discipline fits none of these meanings. There is nothing paradoxical about it. So our revision can bleep "paradoxically" entirely. It just ain't so.

OK. Back to this chapter's main argument. I've asked students repeatedly how they read large stretches of "Official Style" academic prose; the uniform answer has been "I skip from key term to key term and guess at their connection." I've tried to depict this habit in the next sentence:

> The idea of **action language implies** as the correct approach to the emotions **foregoing** the use of **substantives** in making **emotion-statements** and **employing** for this purpose only **verbs and adverbs** or adverbial locutions.

We might call this "highlighter reading"; it can provide a handy guide for revision. It may someday find its way into the printing conventions for wallboard prose like this, as a kind of running internal summary. Probably, though, it would prove too satirical. Try using the "highlights" as the starting point for a revision and see what you come up with.

In the following typographical rendering, I've tried to depict visually a sentence slowly running out of gas as it passes through its prepositional-phrase string. I've used italics at the end to emphasize how the vital concept in the sentence—compassionate service—has been placed in the least emphatic place possible, just before the sentence peters out completely.

Dr. Heartfelt has earned a
reputation for excellence for the sharing of the
wisdom of the path of *compassionate service* in the natural
healing arts.

Diagramming prose rhythm in a printed book, though, never works well; it goes against the grain of the medium. Examples like this should put the shrinkage *in action*.

REFLECTIONS ON THE ELECTRONIC WORD

I've presented these typographical transformations as tools of analysis, but they are tools of creation as well. And the creative revolution in prose expression will only continue to expand.

Text has, for a start, been put into a *three-dimensional* field. Imagine text floating in space, with a reader flying through this space, going ever deeper into the text. Imagine a text with its general arguments at the surface and the supporting detail existing in smaller and smaller scale as you fly through the space. Three-dimensional textual space may sound odd, but we already talk about text *metaphorically* in this way: We say we are "going deeper" into a text, "getting to the bottom" of an argument, or have "skimmed the surface" of a report.

In addition to being put back into space, text has been put back into time. A mode of presentation called "kinetic typography," long common in TV ads, presents text in real time, word or phrase at a time, swimming forward to our eyes or receding from them. This textual animation blends typographic design with choreography—the type begins to dance.

I have no idea where this cornucopia of changes will fetch us up, but clearly prose, and prose revision, will never be the same. Revising the electronic word will be easier, more challenging, creative, and much more fun. The kind of typographical manipulation and commentary we've been toying with sketches the coming metamorphosis of the word. With it will come a new understanding of prose style and, indeed, a new definition of prose itself. The electronic word has changed the whole matrix of written expression, just as digitization has transformed the marketplace itself. To ignore this state-change at the one level is as perilous as to ignore it at the other.

The logic of an attention economy will lead us to a self-consciousness about words and the signals they broadcast far greater than is now customary. The kind of verbal self-consciousness now restricted to writers and literary critics will, by the technological "logic" of an electronic information society, become a core professional skill. That new conception of prose—as wide as language itself, and as bright and sparkling and changeable as the electronic word can make it—offers a new and lively path whose ending none of us can foresee. The Official Style—shapeless, voiceless, confusing and confused—will find itself under competitive market pressures when it walks this path. We'll resent its ugliness as much as its inefficiency. These competitive pressures offer new reasons we should bother to revise it.

8

Why Bother?

Revising Prose argues that the Official Style muddles much American prose—and, since English has become a world language, the world's prose as well. To the extent that this is true, the paramedic analogy holds and the prose can be revised using simple procedures. We have illustrated the Official Style's attributes: dominantly a noun style; a concept style; a style whose sentences have no artful design, no rhythm or emphasis; a voiceless, impersonal style; a style built on euphemism; a style with a formulaic sentence structure, "is" plus a string of prepositional phrases before and after. And we've learned how to revise it. A set of do-it-yourself techniques, the Paramedic Method, handles the problem nicely, if sometimes laboriously. But at this point you may well be asking, "Why bother?" Why see in a blind world? Why spend extra time making yourself conspicuous? There are two answers, or rather two kinds of answer.

THE FIRST KIND OF ANSWER

The first kind: "If you can see what others can't, you'll get ahead." Sometimes this is true and sometimes not. Generally, it helps if you write better prose. It makes for a better statement of purpose when you apply for law school or a job; later on, it will help you write a better legal brief or progress report or memo. Today, when ordinary writing skills are seldom to be found, this holds truer than ever.

Where the Official Style is mandated by rule or custom, however, plain straightforward prose may sound simpleminded or even flip. The sensible procedure: Learn both languages, the plain and the Official Style. As always in the two millennia of rhetoric's history, there are rules that work but no rules about when to apply those rules. I cannot better the answer that the likes of Aristotle, Cicero, and Quintilian have always returned. Learn the rules and then, through experience, train your intuition to apply them effectively. *Stylistic* judgment is, last as well as first, always *political* judgment. That ineluctable equation—which there is no dodging—makes stylistic judgment vital enough to warrant books like this one.

As a political decision, writing plainly constitutes a better decision today than even half a dozen years ago. We now live, we are told daily, in an information economy. The vital commodity is no longer physical stuff but the information needed to extract it from the earth's crust and process it into goods. But the commodity in short supply—what economists usually study—is not information. We lack not information—we're drowning in that—but the time to make sense of it. The vital commodity turns out to be *human attention*. We might better, as we have seen, call our present situation an attention economy than an information one.

In an economy of attention, a cardinal transformation takes place. In a goods economy, the essential artifact is physical stuff. That stuff provides the controlling value. *Things* dominate. The language that describes those things has value only as it describes the things. The people who deal with things—dig materials from the earth's crust, process those materials, make stuff out of them—occupy center stage. The language used to describe them plays a secondary role. If you can use mathematical formulas, that is best. If you have to use words, use words that point directly to the things. But the *words* rank second to the *things*. In an economy of attention, this relationship inverts. Words *allocate attention*. They mediate between information and the people who use it. Words now occupy center stage, and stuff moves to the wings.

In a goods economy, suppose somebody writes an Official Style sentence that takes too long to tell its tale, and confuses the tale into the bargain. Well, so what? The stuff gets through, and that's the important thing. If you can save time and money *making the stuff,* good for you. That matters. But nobody saves any real money making *words* more efficient. They play a derivative role. This assumption profoundly mistakes how even a goods economy works, as our revisions in earlier chapters have shown. But the same assumption proves catastrophic in an economy of attention. When you waste words, you are wasting the principal scarce resource—attention. The Official Stylist wastes his own attention in adding lard, but he wastes the reader's attention as well. Attention is what *adds value* in an attention economy. The pompous posturing of the Official Style attacks productivity at its heart—where data are converted into productive, usable, information.

We can now introduce the most compelling reason the Official Style continues to thrive. *Because we really don't think words matter.* They don't matter enough to make instruction in them an essential concern. And so we train ourselves not to pay attention to them. Writing badly becomes almost a matter of pride; hire someone else to do it if you can't. A great deal of pious cant today proclaims that writing is important, but we don't really believe it. In an economy of attention you had better believe it. There, words matter.

This change from stuff to attention is creating strong pressures to write in the plain style. We've just discussed some of these pressures in the previous chapter. To take one example, the Securities and Exchange Commission has issued a special set of guidelines—readers of *Revising Prose* will find them familiar—for the preparation of documents being submitted to that agency. The agency will no longer tolerate (at least, so it says) the enormous expenditure of attention required to decode the Official Style. All across our economy, extraordinary efforts have been made to cut costs and reduce waste. It should not surprise us when the Official Style catches the cost-cutters' gaze. Precisely the revision *Revising Prose* teaches has become a valuable talent, not simply an elegant adornment.

THE SECOND KIND OF ANSWER

The second kind of answer to "Why bother?" is both simpler than the first and more complex. We've looked at many examples of inept writing—writing that ranges from shapeless to mindless. The second kind of answer to "Why bother?" is simply, "Are you willing to sign your name to what you have written? To present yourself in public—whether it matters to anyone else or not—as such a person?" In a sense, it is a simple question: "Whatever the advantage—or disadvantage—ought I do this?" The primary moral question: If everyone else is committing perjury, ought I do the same? This is not a theoretical question: American businesses and American politics have faced it repeatedly in recent times. Do you choose to encounter the world on its terms or on your own? Are you willing to sign off on a fraudulent balance sheet, private or public, simply because others do it? Sign off on a piece of writing that does not mean what it says, or worse, not know what it means, that wastes the reader's time because you are unwilling to spend your own? A simple question but one we must all answer for ourselves.

"The style is the man," says the old adage. Perhaps it means that to this basic moral question you'll give the same answer for writing as for the rest of your behavior. Yet the question is complex, too, for what kind of behavior is "prose behavior"? Prose is usually described in a moral vocabulary—"sincere," "open," "devious," "hypocritical"—but is this vocabulary justified? Why, for that matter, has it been so moralistic? And why, in fact, do we think "bad" the right word to use for it?

STYLE AND SELF

Let's start with the primary ground for morality, the self. We may think of the self as both a dynamic and a static entity. It is static when we think of ourselves as having central, fixed selves independent of our surroundings, an "I" we can remove from society without damage, a central self inside our head. But it becomes dynamic when we think of ourselves as actors playing social roles, a series of roles that vary with the social situation in which we find ourselves. Such a social self amounts to the sum of all the public roles we play. Our complex identity comes from the constant interplay of these two kinds of self. Our final "self" is usually a mixed one, few of us being completely the same in all situations or, conversely, social chameleons who change with every context. The self grows and develops through the free interplay between these two kinds of self. If we were completely sincere we would always say exactly what we think—and cause social chaos. If we were always acting an appropriate role, we would be certifiably insane. Reality, for each of us, presents itself as constant oscillation between these two extremes.

When we say that writing is sincere, we mean that somehow it has managed to express this complex oscillation, this complex self. It has caught the accent of a particular self, a particular mixture of the two selves. Sincerity can't point to any specific verbal configuration, since sincerity varies as widely as human beings themselves. The sincere writer has not said exactly what she felt in the first words that occurred to her. That might produce a revolutionary tirade, or "like, you know" conversational babble, or the gross mistakes we've been reviewing. Nor has a sincere writer simply borrowed a fixed language, as when a bureaucrat writes in the Official Style. She has managed to create a style which, like the social self, can become part of society, can work harmoniously in society and, at the same time, like the central self, can represent her unique selfhood. She holds her two selves in balance; this is what "authority" in prose means.

Now reverse this process. Writing prose involves for the writer an integration of self, a deliberate act of balancing its two component parts. It represents an act of socialization, and it is by repeated acts of socialization that we become sociable beings, that we grow up. Thus, the act of writing models the presentation of self in society; prose reality rehearses us for social reality. It models how we behave there. It is not a question of a preexistent self making its message known to a preexistent society. It is not, initially, a question of message at all. Writing clarifies, strengthens, and energizes the self, renders individuality rich, full, and social. This does not mean writing that flows, as Terry Southern immortally put it, "right out of the old guts onto the goddamn paper." Precisely the opposite. Only by taking the position of the reader toward one's own prose, putting a reader's pressure on it, can the self be made to grow into full sociability. Writing should enhance and expand the self, allow it to try out new possibilities, tentative selves.

The moral ingredient in writing, then, works first not on the morality of the message but on the nature of the sender, on the complexity of the self. "Why bother?" To invigorate and enrich your selfhood, to increase, in the most literal sense, your self-consciousness. Writing, properly pursued, does not make you better. It makes you more alive. This is why our growing illiteracy ought to distress us. It tells us something, something alarming, about the impoverishment of our selves. We say that we fear written communication will break down. Unlikely. And if it does we can always do what we do anyway—pick up the phone or get on the web. Something more fundamental stands at stake, the selfhood and sociability of the communicators. We are back to the basic peculiarity of writing: It is premeditated utterance, and in that premeditation lives its first if not its only value. "Why bother?" "To find out who I really am." It is not only what we *think* that we discover in writing, but what we *are* and *can construct ourselves to be*.

We can now understand why the purely neutral, transparent style is so hard to write and so rare, and why we take to jargon, to the Official Style, to all the varieties of poetic diction and verbal ornament, with such alacrity. We are doing more in writing, any writing, than transmitting neutral messages. We want to convey our feelings about what we say, our attitude toward the human relationships we are establishing. Neutral communications do not come naturally to people. What matters most to us is our relationships with our fellow creatures. These urges continually express themselves through what we write. They energize what we call style. Style has attracted a moralistic vocabulary because it expresses all the patterns of human behavior that morality must control. This moralistic vocabulary leads to considerable confusion, but it arises naturally enough from the way human beings use literary style.

How rare a purely neutral human relationship really is you can appreciate simply by reflecting on your daily life. Is there any response, however trivial, that we don't color with hand gestures, facial expressions, postures of the body? Human beings are nonstop expressors, often through minute subconscious clues. We sense, immediately, that a friend is angry at us by the way he says "Hello." He doesn't say, "Go to hell, you skunk" instead of "Hello." He doesn't need to. Tense vocal chords, pursed lips, a curt bob of the head perhaps, do just as well. No one has put a percentage figure to this segment of human communication, but it far outranks plain statement in frequency and importance. The same truth prevails for written communication. We are always trying to say more than we actually do. This stylistic voice-over technique is our natural way of speaking. *Skotison* makes perfect sense when we consider the entire range of human expression.

VALUE JUDGMENTS

We now begin to understand what kinds of value judgments make sense about prose and what kinds don't. The prevailing wisdom teaches that the best prose style is the most transparent, the least seen; prose ideally aspires to a perfect neutrality; like the perfect secretary, it gets the job done without intruding. Such ideal prose rarely occurs. Might that be because it isn't ideal? Doesn't ideal neutrality rule out most of what we call good prose? The ideal document of perfect neutrality would be a grocery list. (And think of how we immediately flood that neutral document with likes and dislikes, with *emotions*—not sardines *again!*) We mean by "good prose" something different from impersonal transparency. We mean a style suffused with a sense of human relationships, of specific occasions and why they matter. We mean a style that expresses a genuinely complex and fully socialized self.

We've cleared up a lot of muddy writing in this book. The metaphor "clear up" is clear enough, and there is no reason not to use it, but I can now explain more precisely what we have been doing. An incoherent style is "clear enough." It depicts clearly an incoherent mind, an incoherent person. Looked at in this way, all prose is clear. Revision aims to "clear up" the *person*, to present a self more coherent, more in control. A mind thinking, not a mind asleep. It aims, that is, not to denature the human relationship that prose sets up, but to enhance and enrich it. It tries not to squeeze out the expression of personality but to make this expression possible, not to squeeze out all record of a particular occasion and its human relationships but to make them maximally clear. Again, this is why we (well, at least some of us) worry so much about bad prose. It signifies incoherent people, failed social relationships. This worry makes sense only if we feel that prose, ideally, should express human relationships and feelings, not abolish them.

Think, for example, about a familiar piece of prose we might all call successful, Lincoln's *Gettysburg Address*. Its brevity has been much praised, but the brevity does not work in a vacuum. It makes sense, becomes expressive, only in relation to the occasion. Lincoln took for his subject the inevitable gap between words and deeds. At Gettysburg, this gap was enormous, and the shortness of Lincoln's speech does reverence to it. No speech could do justice to what had happened at Gettysburg. Lincoln's brevity did not remove the emotion of the occasion but intensified it; it did not ignore the occasion's human relationships but celebrated them. We think it a monument to brevity and clarity not because it neutralizes human emotion but because it so superbly enshrines the emotions that fit the occasion.

Human beings are social beings. Our reality is a social reality. Our identity draws its felt life from our relation to other people. We become uneasy if, for extended periods of time, we neither hear nor see other people. We feel uneasy with the Official Style for the same reason. It has no human voice, no face, no personality behind it. It creates no society, encourages no social conversation. We feel that it is unreal. The "better" it is, the more typical, the more unreal it becomes. And so we can answer the question of whether you can write a "good" Official Style. Yes, of course, when you must work in the Official Style, you can observe its conventions in a minimal way. But the closer you get to the impersonal essence of the Official Style, the more distant any felt human reality becomes.

It is a bad style, then, because it denatures human relations. When we consider that it has become the accepted language for most of the organizations that govern our human relations, we perceive how stylistic and moral issues converge. Our current literacy crisis may have come from more than inattention, laziness, or even the obfuscatory purposes of the Official Style. It may stem, ultimately, from our meager ideal for prose. We say that what we want is only a serviceable tool—useful, durable, honest, practical, and so on. But none of us takes so utilitarian an attitude even toward our tools! If we earn our living with them, we love them. We clean and polish and lubricate them. We prefer one kind to another for quirky, personal reasons. We modify them. We want them not only to do a job but also to express us, the attitude we take toward our job.

So, too, with prose. We hunger for ceremony, for attitude, for ornament. It is no accident that bureaucrats play games with buzz-words, build what amounts to purely ornamental patterns, create a *poetic* diction. These games express an attitude, albeit an ironically despairing one, toward what they are doing, the spirit in which they work. Jargons are created, too, for the same reason, to express a mystique, the spirit in which work is done. And, like a student's incoherence, they have their own eloquence, reflect clearly a habit of thought, a way of doing business. When we object to the prose, we are actually objecting to the habit of thought, the bureaucratic habits of thought and way of life. It is because, paradoxically enough, the style is so clear, so successfully communicates a style of life, that we so feel its emotional impoverishment.

"No Profit Is Where Is No Pleasure Taken"

We have two choices, then, in writing and revising prose. We can allow the expression of personality and social relationships and attempt to control them, or we can ban them and try to extinguish them. Perhaps we should try the first alternative for a while. We've tried the second for more than century and we know where it leads. It leads to where we are now, to the Official Style.

For those of us working alone to improve our prose, the choice is even clearer. Even if society disregards the importance of words, we must go in the other direction, train ourselves to notice them and to notice them as much as their "content." A style that at first appears peculiar may not be a "bad" style but simply eloquent about an unexpected slice of reality, one that you may or may not like. Keep clear in mind when you are responding to the words and when to the situation they represent. You'll find that you do first the one and then the other. You'll be rehearsing the same oscillation we have already found to be at the base of stylistic revision. You'll have trained your pattern of attention in the same way that an artist trains his eyes or a musician her ears. After all, you can't revise what you can't see. Only by sensitizing yourself to the styles around you can you go beyond a fixed set of rules, a paramedic procedure.

In fact, in the long run, that is what any fixed set of rules ideally ought to do. It ought to guide us in training our verbal vision, expanding our intuition about words. Rules, analytic devices, are a shortcut to vision but no real substitute for being able to *see* a prose pattern. The paramedic analogy here breaks down. Beyond paramedicine lies medicine; beyond the specific analysis of specific styles—what we have been doing here—lies the study of style in general. Verbal style can no more be fully explained by a set of rules, stylistic or moral, than can the rest of human behavior. Intuition, trained intuition, figures equally strongly in both. You must learn how to see, and that learning is not entirely a rule-based proceeding.

Prose style, then, cannot be reduced to a set of simple rules about clarity, brevity, and sincerity. It is as complicated as the rest of human behavior because it forms part of that behavior as well as expressing it. Anyone who tells you that mastering prose style is simple is kidding you. As students, all of us often complain about the "unreality" of our school life, but where school life at any level is most real—in the vital act of verbal expression—we most yearn for simplification. Well, we can't have it both ways. You can choose the moralizing, rule-centered world, with its simplistic static conception of self and society, but you must not be surprised, when you use it in the real world, if it seems "unreal" in theory and backfires in practice.

The other road is harder. You have to read and write and pay attention to both acts. If you do, you'll begin to savor the elegance with which we humans can communicate the subtleties of behavior. You'll begin to become self-conscious about the language you speak and hence about the society you live in. You will become more alive. And you'll begin to suspect what is perhaps a third answer to the question, "Why bother?" Because it's more fun.

Terms

You can see things you don't know the names for, but in prose style, as in everything else, it is easier to see what you know how to describe. The psychological ease that comes from calling things by their proper names has not often been thought a useful goal by modern pedagogy. As a result, inexperienced writers often find themselves reduced to talking about "smoothness," "flow," and other meaningless generalities when they are confronted by a text. So here are some basic terms.

PARTS OF SPEECH

In traditional English grammar, there are eight parts of speech: verbs, nouns, pronouns, adjectives, adverbs, prepositions, conjunctions, interjections. *Grammar*, in its most general sense, refers to all the rules that govern how meaningful statements can be made in any language. *Syntax* refers to sentence structure, to word order. *Diction* means simply word choice. *Usage* means linguistic custom.

Verbs

1. Verbs have two voices, active and passive.
   An *active verb* indicates the subject acting:
   Jack *kicks* Bill.

A *passive verb* indicates the subject acted upon:

Bill *is kicked by* Jim.

2. Verbs come in three moods: indicative, subjunctive, and imperative.

A verb in the *indicative mood* says that something is a fact. If it asks a question, it is a question about a fact:

Jim kicks Bill. Has Bill kicked Jim yet?

A verb in the *subjunctive mood* says that something is a wish, hypothetical, or contrary to fact, rather than a fact:

If Jim *were* clever, he would kick Bill.

A verb in the *imperative mood* issues a command:

Jim, *kick* Bill.

3. A verb can be either transitive or intransitive.

A *transitive* verb takes a direct object:

Jim *kicks* Bill.

An *intransitive* verb does not take a direct object. It represents action without a specific goal:

Lori *runs* every day.

The verb "to be" ("is," "was," and so on) is often a linking verb because it links subject and predicate without expressing a specific action:

Elaine *is* a movie mogul.

4. English verbs have six tenses: present, past, present perfect, past perfect, future, and future perfect.

Present: Jim *kicks* Bill.

Past: Jim *kicked* Bill.

Present perfect: Jim *has kicked* Bill.

Past perfect: Jim *had kicked* Bill.

Future: Jim *will kick* Bill.

Future perfect: Jim *will have kicked* Bill.

The present perfect, past perfect, and future perfect are called compound tenses. Each tense can have a progressive form (e.g., present progressive: Jim *is kicking* Bill.).

5. Verbs in English have three so-called infinitive forms: *infinitive, participle,* and *gerund.* These verb forms often function as adjectives or nouns.

Infinitive:

> *To assist* Elaine isn't easy.

Participles and gerunds have the same form; when the form is used as an adjective, it is called a *participle*, when used as a noun, a *gerund*.

Participles:

Present participle:
> Elaine was in an *arguing* mood.

Past participle:
> Lori's presentation was very well *argued*.

Gerund:

> *Arguing* with Elaine is no fun.

(When a word separates the "to" in an infinitive from its complementary form, as in "to directly stimulate" instead of "to stimulate," the infinitive is said to be a split infinitive. Most people think this separation is something we should avoid if possible.)

Verbs that take "it" or "there" as subjects are said to be in an impersonal construction: "It has been decided to fire him" or "There has been a personnel readjustment."

Nouns

A noun names something or somebody. A proper noun names a particular being or place—Elaine, Secretariat, Titanic, Pittsburgh—and is capitalized.

1. *Number.* The singular number refers to one ("a cat"), plural to more than one ("five cats").
2. *Collective nouns.* Groups may be thought of as a single unit, as in "the army," and thus take a singular verb. "The army is severely understrength."

Pronouns

A pronoun is a word that replaces a noun. There are different kinds:

1. *Personal pronouns*: I, me, him . . .
2. *Intensive pronouns*: myself, yourself . . .

3. *Relative pronouns:* who, which, that. These must have antecedents, words they refer back to. "Lori has a talent (antecedent) that (relative pronoun) Elaine does not possess."
4. *Indefinite pronouns:* somebody, anybody, anything
5. *Interrogative pronouns:* who?, what?

Adjectives

An *adjective* modifies a noun: "Lori was a *good* hiker."

Adverbs

An *adverb* modifies a verb: "Lori hiked *swiftly* up the trail." "Jim kicked Bill *hard.*"

Prepositions

A *preposition* connects a noun or pronoun with a verb, an adjective, or another pronoun: "I ran *into* her arms" or "The girl *with* the blue scarf."

Conjunctions

Conjunctions join sentences or parts of them. There are two kinds: coordinating and subordinating.

1. *Coordinating conjunctions*—and, but, or—connect statements of equal status "Bill ran *and* Jim fell" or "I got up *but* soon fell down again."
2. *Subordinating conjunctions*—that, when, because—connect a main clause with a subordinate one: "I thought *that* they had left."

Interjection

A sudden outcry: "Wow!" or "Ouch!"
And a reminder about *possessives*:
Singular: A *worker's* hat. Plural: The *workers'* hats.

("It's," however, equals "it is." **The possessive is "its"—no apostrophe!**)

SENTENCES

Every sentence must have both a subject and verb, stated or implied: "Elaine (subject) directs (verb)."

Three Kinds

1. A *declarative sentence* states a fact: "Elaine directs films."
2. An *interrogative sentence* asks a question: "Does Elaine direct films?"
3. An *exclamatory sentence* registers an exclamation: "Does she ever!"

Three Basic Structures

1. A simple sentence makes one self-standing assertion (i.e., has one main clause: "Elaine directs films.").
2. A compound sentence makes two or more self-standing assertions (i.e., has two or more main clauses: "Elaine directs films and Lori is a tax lawyer" or "Jim kicks Bill and Bill feels it and Bill kicks Jim back.").
3. A complex sentence makes one self-standing assertion and one or more dependent assertions in the form of subordinate clauses dependent on the main clause: "Elaine, who has just finished directing Jim Kicks Bill, must now consult Lori about her tax problems before she can start blocking out Being Kicked: The Sequel."

In *compound sentences*, the clauses are connected by *coordinating conjunctions*, in *complex sentences* by *subordinating conjunctions*.

Restrictive and Nonrestrictive Relative Clauses

A *restrictive clause* modifies directly, and so restricts the meaning of the antecedent it refers back to: "This is the tire *that blew out on the freeway*." One specific tire is referred to. In such clauses the relative clause is not set off by a comma.

A *nonrestrictive clause*, though still a dependent clause, does not directly modify its antecedent and is set off by commas. "These tires, *which are quite expensive*, never blow out on the freeway."

Appositives

An *appositive* is an amplifying word or phrase placed next to the term it refers to and set off by commas: "Henry VIII, *a glutton for punishment*, rode out hunting even when sick and in pain."

BASIC SENTENCE PATTERNS

What words do you use to describe the basic syntactic patterns in a sentence? In addition to the basic types, declarative, interrogative, and exclamatory, and the basic forms of simple, compound, and complex, other terms sometimes come in handy.

Parataxis and Hypotaxis

Parataxis: Phrases or clauses arranged independently, in a coordinate construction, and often without connectives (e.g., "I came, I saw, I conquered.").

Hypotaxis: Phrases or clauses arranged in a dependent subordinate relationship (e.g., "I came, and after I came and looked around a bit, I decided, well, why not, and so conquered.").

The adjectival forms are *paratactic* and *hypotactic* (e.g., "Hemingway favors a paratactic syntax while Faulkner prefers a hypotactic one.").

Asyndeton and Polysyndeton

Asyndeton: Connectives are omitted between words, phrases, or clauses (e.g., "I've been stressed, destressed, beat down, beat up, held down, held up, conditioned, reconditioned.").

Polysyndeton: Connectives are always supplied between words and phrases, or clauses, as when Milton talks about Satan pursuing his way, "And swims, or sinks, or wades, or creeps, or flies."

The adjectives are *asyndetic* and *polysyndetic.*

Periodic Sentence

A periodic sentence is a long sentence with a number of elements, usually balanced or antithetical, standing in a clear syntactical relationship to each other. Usually it suspends the conclusion of the sense until the end of the sentence, and so is sometimes said to use a *suspended syntax.* A periodic sentence shows us a pattern of thought that has been fully worked out, whose power relationships of subordination have been carefully determined, and whose timing has been climactically ordered. In a periodic sentence, the mind has finished working on the thought, left it fully formed.

There is no equally satisfactory antithetical term for the opposite kind of sentence, a sentence whose elements are loosely related to one another, follow in no particularly antithetical climactic order, and do not suspend its grammatical completion until the close. Such a style is often called a *running style* or a *loose style*, but the terms remain pretty vague. The loose style, we can say, often reflects a mind *in the process of thinking* rather than, as in the periodic sentence, having already completely ordered its thinking. A sentence so loose as to verge on incoherence, grammatical or syntactical, is often called a *run-on sentence.*

Isocolon

The Greek word *isocolon* means, literally, syntactic units of equal length, and it is used in English to describe the repetition of phrases of approximately equal length and corresponding structure. Preachers, for example, often depend on isocolon to build up a rhythmic pattern or develop a series of contrasting ideas. Winston Churchill used *isocolon* in describing the life of a politician: "He is asked to stand, he wants to sit, and he is expected to lie."

Chiasmus

Chiasmus is the basic pattern of antithetical inversion, the AB:BA pattern. President John Kennedy used it in his inaugural address:

A	B
Ask not what your country	*can do for you, but*

B	A
what you can do	*for your country.*

Anaphora

When you begin a series of phrases, clauses, or sentences with the same word or phrase, you are using anaphora. So Shakespeare's Henry V to some henchpersons who have betrayed him:

> Show men dutiful?
> *Why, so didst thou.* Seem they grave and learned?
> *Why, so didst thou.* Come they of noble family?
> *Why, so didst thou.* Seem they religious?
> *Why, so didst thou.*
>
> (*Henry V*, II, ii)

Tautology

Repetition of the same idea in different words. In many ways, the Official Style is founded on this pattern. Here's a neat example from Shakespeare:

> *Lepidus.* What manner o'thing is your crocodile?
> *Antony.* It is shap'd, sir, like itself, and it is as broad as it has breadth. It is just so high as it is, and moves with its own organs. It lives by that which nourisheth it, and the elements once out of it, it transmigrates.
> *Lepidus.* What colour is it of?
> *Antony.* Of its own colour too.

Lepidus. 'Tis a strange serpent.
Antony. 'Tis so. And the tears of it are wet.

(*Antony and Cleopatra*, II, vii)

Noun Style and Verb Style

Every sentence must have a noun and a verb, but one can be emphasized, sometimes almost to the exclusion of the other. The Official Style—strings of prepositional phrases + "is"—exemplifies a noun style *par excellence*. Here are three examples, the first of a noun style, the second of a verb style, and the third of a balanced noun-verb mixture.

NOUN STYLE

There is in turn a two-fold structure of this "binding-in." In the first place, by virtue of internalization of the standard, conformity with it tends to be of personal, expressive and/or instrumental significance to ego. In the second place, the structuring of the reactions of alter to ego's action as sanctions is a function of his conformity with the standard. Therefore conformity as a direct mode of the fulfillment of his own need-dispositions tends to coincide with the conformity as a condition of eliciting the favorable and avoiding the unfavorable reactions of others.

(Talcott Parsons, *The Social System* [Glencoe, Ill.: Free Press, 1951], p. 38)

VERB STYLE

Patrols, sweeps, missions, search and destroy. It continued every day as if part of sunlight itself. I went to the colonel's briefings every day. He explained how effectively we were keeping the enemy off balance, not allowing them to move in, set up mortar sites, and gather for attack. He didn't seem to hate them. They were to him like pests or insects that had to be kept away. It seemed that one important purpose of patrols was just for them to take place, to happen, to exist; there had to be patrols. It gave the men something to do. Find the enemy, make contact, kill, be killed, and return. Trap, block, hold. In the first five days, I lost six corpsmen—two killed, four wounded.

(John A. Parrish, *12, 20 & 5: A Doctor's Year in Vietnam* [Baltimore: Penguin Books, 1973], p. 235)

MIXED NOUN-VERB STYLE

We know both too much and too little about Louis XIV ever to succeed in capturing the whole man. In externals, in the mere business of eating, drinking, and dressing in the outward routine of what he loved to call the *metier du roi*, no historical character, not even Johnson or Pepys, is better known to us; we can even, with the aid of his own writings, penetrate a little of the majestic façade which is Le Grand Roi. But when we have done so, we see as in a glass darkly. Hence the extraordinary number and variety of judgments which have been passed upon him; to one school, he is incomparably the ablest ruler in modern European history; to another, a mediocre blunderer, pompous, led by the nose by a succession of generals and civil servants; whilst to a third, he is no great king, but still the finest actor of royalty the world has ever seen.

(W. H. Lewis, *The Splendid Century: Life in the France of Louis XIV* [N.Y.: Anchor Books, 1953], p. 1)

PATTERNS OF RHYTHM AND SOUND

Meter

The terms used for scanning (marking the meter of) poetry sometimes prove useful for prose as well.

> *iamb*: unstressed syllable followed by a stressed one (e.g., in vólve)
> *trochee*: opposite of iamb (e.g., ám ber)
> *anapest*: two unstressed syllables and one stressed syllable (e.g., there he góes)
> *dactyl*: opposite of anapest, one stressed syllable followed by two unstressed ones (e.g., óp er ate)

These patterns form *feet*. If a line contains two, it is a *dimeter*; three, a *trimeter*; four, a *tetrameter*; five, a *pentameter*; six, a *hexameter*. The adjectival forms are *iambic, trochaic, anapestic,* and *dactylic*.

Sound Resemblances

Alliteration: This originally meant the repetition of initial consonant sounds but came to mean repetition of consonant sounds
wherever they occurred, and now is often used to indicate vowel
sound repetition as well. You can use it as a general term for this
kind of sound play: "Peter Piper picked a peck of pickled pep-
pers"; "Bill will always swill his fill."

For further explanation of the basic terms of grammar, see
Michael Strumpf and Auriel Douglas, *The Grammar Bible* (New
York: Henry Holt, 2004). For a fuller discussion of rhetorical
terms like *chiasmus* and *asyndeton*, see Richard A. Lanham,
A Handlist of Rhetorical Terms, 2nd ed., University of California
Press, 1991. For a fuller discussion of prose style, see Richard A.
Lanham, *Analyzing Prose*, 2nd ed. (London and New York:
Continuum, 2003).

Exercises

Some of these examples were published in a separate booklet to accompany an earlier edition of *Revising Prose*, but I've been persuaded that they would be more conveniently located here. The examples that follow are all real and unaltered. Diagnose the problems illustrated by the example, then try your hand at revision. If you need more space than I've provided for your revision, keep revising.

1. In the case of finding a set of premises that are beyond our limited means of verification, all we can say about the belief we originally set out to judge is that it is as certain, and no more certain, as these fundamental premises are.

Diagnosis:

_____

_____

Revision:

_____

_____

2. The following experiments are reconstructions of those two significant discoveries.

Diagnosis:

_____

_____

Revision:

_____

_____

3. Since I have no plans to write a book about the Weather Service, I will try to be brief, but concise in the ensuing pages.

Diagnosis:

_____

_____

Revision:

_____

_____

4. It must suffice to say that the traditional values, in which the goal is prosperity and stability, eudaimonia, and the agathos, the man whose characteristics are commended by arete, is the prosperous, brave and successful man, are still dominant.

Diagnosis:

_____

_____

Revision:

_____

_____

_____

_____

5. Before 1750 A.D. the world was characterized by the lack of any urbanization.

Diagnosis:

_____

_____

Revision:

_____

_____

6. During the last fifties and early sixties, a phenomenon is taking place in the family for the first time.

Diagnosis:

_____

_____

Revision:

_____

_____

7. For the most part, my relationship with my Mentees has been one of friendship.

Diagnosis:

_____

_____

Revision:

_____

_____

8. One of the most important indicators of the sensorimotor period is the gradual development of object permanence.

Diagnosis:

_____

_____

Revision:

_____

_____

9. A political philosophy that was evident in all stable preindustrial cities was Capitalism.

Diagnosis:

_____

_____

Revision:

_____

_____

10. The excerpt is an increment in the process of informing the reader regarding the characters by permitting the reader to infer from events rather than accept a description.

Diagnosis:

_____

_____

Revision:

_____

_____

_____

11. The notion of a process of abstraction at a perceptual level is not a new one.

Diagnosis:

_____

_____

Revision:

_____

_____

12. An awareness of the role of the recording industry in the dissemination of folk music and musical styles is not new; to date, however, there has been little consideration of the importance of commercial recording in relation to Irish folk music.

Diagnosis:

_____

_____

Revision:

_____

_____

_____

_____

13. By individuals internalizing and conforming to rules which are enforced by authority, a harmonious social structure is maintained.

Diagnosis:

_____

_____

Revision:

_____

_____

14. The manner in which behavior first shown in a conflict situation may become fixed so that it persists after the conflict has passed is then discussed.

Diagnosis:

_____

_____

Revision:

_____

_____

_____

15. Due to the many false connotations radiated throughout Cinderella, this fairy tale may prove to be a influence on children, and harmful to them during the course of their lives.

Diagnosis:

_____

_____

Revision:

_____

_____

_____

16. The differences in the presentation and rehearsal times may also have had some effect on the results.

Diagnosis:

_____

_____

Revision:

_____

_____

17. He is continually obsessed with the longing of death and at times is fascinated with death's peculiar nature.

Diagnosis:

_____

_____

Revision:

_____

_____

18. The lot of the prisoner on the battlefield of the gunpowder age benefited from the generalization of the principle of ransom.

Diagnosis:

_____

_____

Revision:

_____

_____

19. A perfect example of the resultant polluted fragmentation of the Russian intelligentsia may be seen in the characters of Dostoevsky's *The Idiot*, who have a desperate awareness of the uncertain ground of their actions that causes them to hurl themselves towards a decisive event—revolution, crime, suicide, libertinism, religious extremism—in the hope that the external situation thus created will deprive them of choice and impose unity on their personalities.

Diagnosis:

_____

_____

_____

Revision:

_____

_____

_____

_____

20. What I hope to accomplish in this report is threefold.

Diagnosis:

_____

_____

Revision:

_____

_____

21. As noted on the agenda, this is the meeting at which time a Chairman and Vice-Chairman are to be elected for the next two-year period.

Diagnosis:

_____

_____

Revision:

_____

_____

_____

22. This divided direction caused a degree of confusion on my part as to the type and extent of response required.

Diagnosis:

_____

_____

Revision:

_____

_____

23. The appeal of the reply scenario is that it is both simple and plausible. It is simple in that it requires little explanation and almost no ifs, and, or buts in order to jump from diagnosis to prognostication.

Diagnosis:

_____

_____

Revision:

_____

_____

_____

24. It is important to keep in mind that most situational factors represent both an opportunity and a threat to the future health of the organization.

Diagnosis:

_____

_____

Revision:

_____

_____

25. Interrupting meetings or other individual conversations is simply discourteous and must change. We specifically brought this up during your performance review and we have seen virtually no improvement. Related to this is your overall conversational habits which appears as always being on transmit and rarely on receive. That is, you tend to talk to much and listen too little. This not only occurs one on one, but in meetings as well.

Diagnosis:

_____

_____

Revision:

_____

_____

_____

_____

26. It is interesting to contemplate why there are so many players in the defense decision cycle. One answer is that each participating organization plays the role they do because it is the law. That answer is true, but a more insightful observation is that the intensity and visibility with which these roles are played is because that's "where the action is"—or, more to the point, that's where the power is. Defense decisions are budgetary decisions; the defense budget is by far the largest part of the federal budget; and Washington is a city where power and visibility are preeminent. Decision authority over defense resource allocations is power. And it is visible power.

Diagnosis:

_____

_____

Revision:

_____

_____

_____

_____

_____

_____

_____

27. The purpose of this document is to specifically define a plan for marketing retail products and services. All markets undergo an evolutionary unfolding marked by changing customer needs, technologies, competitors, and laws.

Diagnosis:

_____

_____

Revision:

_____

_____

_____

28. There would be meeting after meeting after meeting of whomever with him at which decisions would be not be made with him *at the meeting.*

Diagnosis:

_____

_____

Revision:

_____

_____

29. No Times editor who was asked about Dalton Avenue could recall why the paper didn't react more quickly, but that the first story and the next one - eight days later - were relatively short and written by a summer intern, not a regular reporter.

Diagnosis:

_____

_____

Revision:

_____

_____

30. Theatre of visions is the staging, with live performers, movement and development in such a fashion as to appear a world or reality or the representation of one by an individual of images occurring to that individual and seeming personally important and significant to him (or her) independently of verbal, intellectual or discursive analysis, —meaningful, but quite possibly the unique significations of their meaning.

Diagnosis:

_____

_____

Revision:

_____

_____

_____

31. We cannot not act, we are in a decision-making mode.

Diagnosis:

_____

Revision:

_____

32. There has been a learning process.

Diagnosis:

_____

Revision:

_____

33. I would like to add that the future of this field is beckoning and wrought with extraordinary potentialities.

Diagnosis:

_____

Revision:

_____

34. Anything that looks dimensional are clickable.

Diagnosis:

_____

Revision:

_____

35. The experience of many in dealing with him was they questioned the truthfulness of what he said.

Diagnosis:

_____

Revision:

_____

Index